CW00385881

WALKING IN BRITAIN

Lake District, Northumbria and Co. Durham

Stan Abbott

NEW
ORCHARD

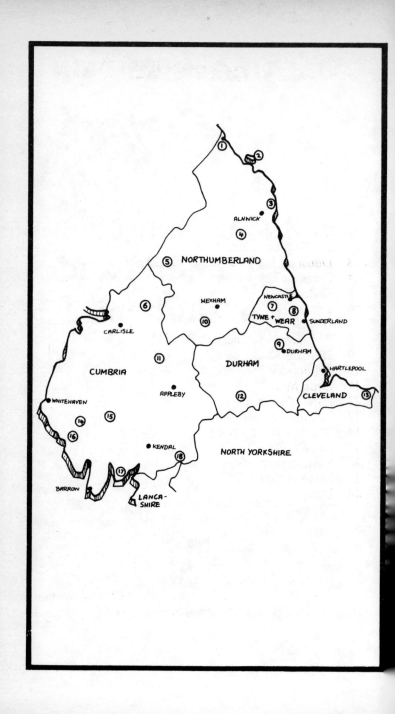

CONTENTS

First published in the UK 1991 by New Orchard Editions
Villiers House, 41/47 Strand, London WC2N 5JE

ISBN 1-85079-170-8

Line drawings by Jill Aldersley
Cartography by Ron Rigby
Photography by David Ward

Printed in Great Britain by Biddles Ltd., Guildford and Kings Lynn

INTRODUCTION

Walking is a pleasure in itself, but it becomes doubly appealing if the route has the objective of visiting a place of special interest. All the walks in this series combine an interesting route with a visit to a well-known feature such as a beauty spot, caves, castle or museum.

The introduction to each walk provides a description of the walk's objective. Most are non-seasonal, and involve little additional walking in themselves once you are there.

Following the description of the objective, each section of the walk is clearly described, and a specially drawn map makes route-finding straightforward. As well as detailing the route, the authors describe many subsidiary points of interest encountered along the way.

The walks are varied and easy to follow. None of them is too taxing, except in the severest weather. Most are circular, returning you to your car at the starting point. Family walkers with young children will find plenty of shorter routes to suit their particular needs, whilst those with longer legs can select from more substantial walks.

The routes have been carefully chosen to include only well-established routes, and readers will certainly increase the enjoyment which they and others derive from the country-side if they respect it by following the Country Code.

Preface and Acknowledgements

Northern England is a vast area of great diversity and includes scenery which is unquestionably among the best in England, if not Britain. The Lake District needs no introduction; the beauties of the Northumberland coast are less loudly proclaimed. Add to them a corner of the limestone dales, the remote Pennines and the "forgotten" valley of the Eden and the challenge becomes for the writer, "What shall I leave out?" In making the choice I have tried to strike a balance, to steer people away from places where tourist numbers are already too pressing and to choose routes which lend themselves well to a circular walk or to public transport access.

Any personal regrets over what has been left out probably relate to the Cheviot Hills and the nearby Kyloe range with the wild cattle of Chillingham, or a city trail through historic Newcastle. I leave these for readers to devise their own routes with the help of the appropriate maps and guides, sticking as ever to the marked rights of way.

It is to be hoped that this book will inspire young and old to leave more often the "mobile prisons" of their cars and take to their feet. Remember as a matter of course – even on the easiest walks – to take a few "iron rations", wear sensible footwear and at least check the *local* weather forecast to ascertain whether waterproofs would be advisable.

I wish to thank Vernon and Dorothy Abbott for their extensive research and legwork, without which this book would not have been possible. Thanks are also due to Alan Earnshaw at Westmorland Visitor Centre and a great many others who helped in many ways. Background information has been drawn from a number of sources which it would be difficult to acknowledge in full.

Stan Abbott

Walk 1
BERWICK TOWN WALLS
NORTHUMBERLAND
4½ miles with 4 miles
of optional detours

Berwick-upon-Tweed, the most northerly town in England, actually lies north of the River Tweed which elsewhere marks the border with Scotland. It still retains its Scottish status as a royal burgh, and the football team plays in the Scottish League. Berwick only finally became part of England late last century after 300 years of neutrality. Once a major port, it handled a fifth of Britain's maritime trade in the thirteenth century, much of it wool from the Tweed valley.

The town is unique in Britain for its massive Elizabethan walls resembling those which ringed continental cities. The old town lies within concentric rings of wall. The first wall – two and a half miles long, 22 feet high and with 19 towers – was built early in the fourteenth century. The second ring was started in 1558, and because by this time artillery had been developed, these walls were built 12 feet thick on the landward side, backed by 30 feet of earth and strengthened by five great bastions known as mounts. Outside the walls is a huge artificial moat up to 200 feet wide, which originally held water. The guns were manned right up to 1908 and through the First World War.

Our walk takes in both old and new walls, as well as the harbourside walls which were remodelled in the eighteenth century, and it includes optional excursions for those wanting a longer stroll.

Leave the A1 at the south end of the by-pass and follow the

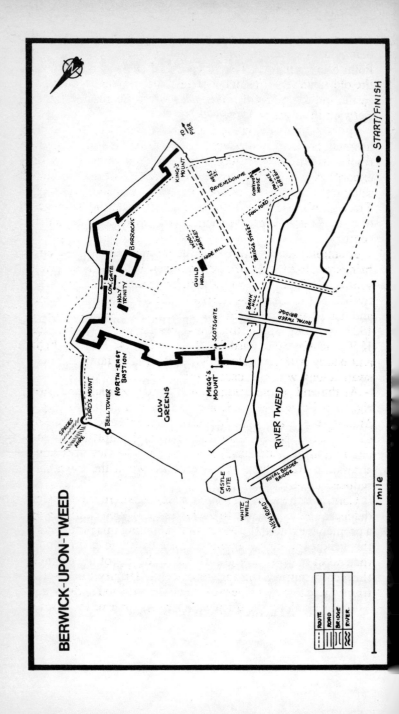

BERWICK-UPON-TWEED

main road into Tweedmouth, descending for half a mile before making a right turn for Spittal. Parking near Sandstell Point offers a fine view over the Tweed to our destination at the old town. Berwick has rail and bus services from Newcastle and Edinburgh, while Spittal can be reached from Berwick by town buses.

Spittal, taking its name from a thirteenth-century leper hospital, last century became a small spa and is still a holiday resort. Most of the fishing and kippering carried out for export has gone, but the fishery protection authorities claim salmon poaching has replaced smuggling as a major industry. The legitimate salmon fishing is effected by netting stretches of river which were apportioned as far back as the twelfth century.

A simple walk of under a mile straight along the shore brings you to the Old Bridge, once guarded by a castle at the south end. This is at least the fifth bridge on the site since the twelfth century and was started in 1611. It is 300 yards long and has 15 arches. On the left is the Royal Tweed Bridge of 1928 and, beyond it, the Royal Border railway bridge of 1850, George Stephenson's 28-arch viaduct, 126 feet high and nearly half a mile long. The river is also famous for its swan colony which is usually 400-strong.

At the end of the bridge (once gated) turn left and fork right up Bank Hill to Scotsgate. On your left is Megg's Mount, the south-west bastion of the Elizabethan walls. Climb on to the wall, cross the old A1 and simply follow the circuit. Past the cattle market and car park the view opens out across the area which was abandoned when the town was reduced in size.

Continue the circuit to King's Mount where the massive defences end to give way to the lower wall which continues as a promenade round the point. Before joining this promenade the walker can detour by making the half-mile excursion to the end of the pier – built in 1810 on the site of the original thirteenth-century one and its sixteenth-century successor – from where there is a fine view down the coast to Lindisfarne.

The walk along the quay walls reveals some of the town's

9

- Berwick on Tweed -

finest old buildings, mostly eighteenth-century, many of which are now being restored. They include the Custom House with its Venetian doorway.

Once back at the Old Bridge end, you can either extend your walk up-river a mile along the New Road, passing below the castle ruins at the White Wall, or begin a tour (described next) of the inner streets by redoubling along Bridge Street. Look out for the famous Cockle Shop which has been making locally renowned sweets since 1801.

Look up Hide Hill, which has several interesting buildings, then turn right down Foul Ford to Palace Green on your left, then left again up Palace Street East and Ravensdowne. There are many things to see here, including the Governor's House, The Main Guard, the old Grammar School and the eighteenth-century houses in Ness Street.

Turn left along Woolmarket to the Guild Hall, whose steeple dominates the main street, and visit the cells in its ancient gaol, if open. The Guild Hall is also a good place for a refreshment stop.

From the lower end of the Guild Hall, turn up Church Street to The Parade where you will find the unusual mid-seventeenth century Holy Trinity Church. Opposite, an ornate gateway leads into the barracks, believed to be Britain's first, which were built to relieve the town of the burden of billeting a large garrison. In 1986 they became home for an art gallery.

Pass from here through the walls to the right by the Cow Gate, turn left to the north-east bastion then follow the remains of the 1310 wall to Lord's Mount at the corner of the old system. From here you can make a detour to the coast by turning right along the Spades Mire ditch and following the top of the fine cliff before returning by the direct path back to the Cow Gate.

You can then return to Spittal via Walkergate and the Royal Tweed Bridge with its fine river views. Alternatively, if you have decided against the coast excursion, continue along the line of the old wall to the prominent Bell Tower and Elizabethan rebuilding then return directly to the Tweed bridge via Low Greens and Scotsgate.

Walk 2
LINDISFARNE CASTLE
NORTHUMBERLAND
4 miles

Islands for many of us hold a peculiar fascination. Although the causeway which is its umbilical to the mainland is submerged only half the time, the Holy Island of Lindisfarne is no exception.

It shares with that other holy isle, Iona in the Hebrides, an atmosphere of tranquillity, serenity almost. But Lindisfarne's history is not purely religious: at the island's southeast corner are reminders of later days of civil war and industrial revolution.

Atop a rugged turret of hard volcanic rock perches our objective, Lindisfarne Castle, plucked straight from the pages of Hans Christian Andersen. The rock was first fortified by the government in 1548 for the defence of Holy Island harbour, a task it performed successfully until 1715 when it was seized briefly by the Stuarts. Its guns were removed in 1819 and the castle lay neglected until 1902 when it was bought by Edward Hudson, the owner of *Country Life*, magazine.

Hudson commissioned Sir Edwin Lutyens, the leading country house architect, to restore the castle and create a comfortable, modern dwelling within the ramparts. Therein lies its appeal: Lindisfarne is surely everybody's dream of a 'castle of their own'. Its fine period furnished rooms are on intriguingly varied levels, and are designed in various shapes, particularly notable being the Ship Room with its vaulted ceiling. The roof is of red pantiles in the tradition of the

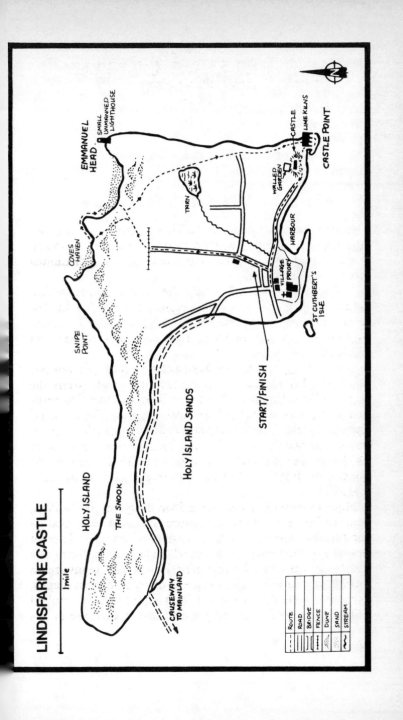

north-east coast, and views from the battlements across to Bamburgh, the Farnes and to the priory are spectacular.

The island is reached via the A1 from either north or south, the latter approach giving, on a clear day, a preview of both Bamburgh Castle and Lindisfarne many miles from Beal, the turn-off for the island. A bus runs from Berwick to a time-table dictated by the tide.

At the start of the causeway a notice board gives drivers the chance to make a last check on crossing times before striking over the sands. These can be checked in either the *Newcastle Journal* or the *Northumberland Gazette*. The ideal day for visiting is when high tide comes soon after mid-day and the crossing can be made in the morning and the return as the water recedes again.

Lindisfarne Castle is open daily except Friday, April to September, and weekends only in October. Winter access, for parties only, by prior arrangement. The Castle Point lime kilns are open all the time and there is no access charge.

Drivers should turn left in the village and use the ample car park there. Our walk encircles the square-mile of rock which forms the main part of the island and also touches a contrasting area of coarse-grassed sand dunes typical of the whole two-mile-long promontory, The Snook, which points towards the mainland.

Turning left out of the car park, away from the village, follow the track north towards The Links. The land on either side is cultivated, but after about three quarters of a mile a fence is reached, beyond which the dunes take over. Through the gate, the track bears right and the walker is advised to follow the defined route to the foot of the dunes proper. Here, keeping the large white beacon on Emmanuel Head well to the right, strike half-left through the dunes by the established paths.

These are shifting sands and erosion is minimised by walkers not creating fresh routes. The area is a nature reserve and among the eel and marram grasses are tiny flowers such as pearlwort, kidney-vetch, lady's bedstraw, the brilliant blue forget-me-not and the pink bog pimpernel. The grasses

14

Lindisfarne

provide food for a rich variety of wintering fowl including wigeon, mallard, geese, dunlin, redshank, eider and rare swans.

We are heading for the shore at Coves Haven, the western-most of two sandy bays sheltered by limestone promontories, which, north wind permitting, makes an excellent picnic spot, sometimes enjoyed by grey seals as well as humans. Then, follow the shore – tide permitting – or strike back along your track until any of a number of vantage points on the dune tops reveals the distinct line of the old waggonway along the eastern shore; head for this. The dunes have buried the old quarry at the northern end of the line which once supplied limestone to the fascinating complex of kilns at Castle Point.

Halfway along this easy mile the walker passes a small tarn where waterfowl can again be watched. When almost at the castle, bear left and follow the path to the beach where the magnificent limekilns have been renovated. The castle entrance is reached by retracing your steps a short way, past the upturned cobles which now form the typical Holy Island fisherman's tackle hut, and up the cobbled way which clings to the precipitous ramparts with their rock plants and fulmar petrel nest sites.

After checking with the castle warden, you can visit the little walled garden created by Gertrude Jeckyll, and recently replanted to her original design after her plan was unearthed in the USA.

Having visited the castle, walk to the village by the track along the shore, past the harbour. Here are the ruins of the eleventh-century Benedictine priory built on the site of the monastery founded by St Aidan in 635 after he was invited from Iona by King Oswald of Northumbria to teach the gospel to his people. In the Norman church can be seen copies of the calligrapher Eadfrid's illuminated Lindisfarne Gospels.

The Lindisfarne Liqueur Company, making mead to a traditional recipe of the monks, has its own factory shop in the village. There is a good choice of pubs, cafes and tea rooms for an island with so small a resident population, and the local delicacies are, of course, crab and lobster.

If tide timings dictate, the walk can equally be carried out in reverse, and there is parking permitted close to the castle for a small fee.

Walk 3
DUNSTANBURGH CASTLE
NORTHUMBERLAND
9¼ or 7 or 5 miles

There can be few sights to rival the ruins of Dunstanburgh Castle for sheer romance. The turrets of its imposing keep, standing proud atop a great promontory of this coast's distinctive whinstone, still bear the scars of civil war. On a typical day of North Sea fret it looms out of the mist like some ghost of history.

Begun in 1316 by Thomas, Earl of Lancaster, the castle – enclosing 11 tussocky acres within its walls – was completed by his successor, John of Gaunt. Apart from the obvious ravages of cannon fire, the sandstone walls of the keep have been etched by wind and rain. To seaward, the plunging cliffs are home for many birds whose screams and the thrashing of the breakers below complete the wild image of Dunstanburgh in such contrast to the civilised serenity of Lindisfarne Castle described elsewhere in this book. Check opening times with the information centre in Craster.

This excursion from Craster forms the heart of an 'elastic' walk, on this dramatic coastline, which can be stretched or shrunk to taste. Craster is a very attractive fishing village of red pantile roofs. Its little harbour is home for about four cobles, the traditional north-east inshore fishing craft which is descended directly from the Viking longboat.

Worth a visit, if such things are to your taste, is the shell museum at Chough's Cafe which has hundreds of models made from locally collected shells. And when the herring are in season, see the kippery where the fish are smoked over

DUNSTANBURGH CASTLE

1 mile

NORTH SEA

LOW NEWTON-BY-THE-SEA

TO SEAHOUSES

TO A1

BIRD HIDE

TARN

B1339

Optional Detour

DUNES

EMBLETON BURN

EMBLETON

DUNSTANBURGH CASTLE

BURN

SIGNPOSTED PATH AT BEND BY WOOD

PATH

TO ALNWICK

B1340

TRACK

LOOKOUT POLE X

ROAD

PROCTORS STEAD FARM

HARBOUR

CRASTER SOUTH FARM

START/FINISH CARPARK + INFORMATION CENTRE

CULLERNOSE POINT

OPTIONAL DETOUR

HOWICK HALL

HAIRPIN

TO LONGHOUGHTON

RUMBLING KERN

	ROUTE
	ROAD
	BRIDGE
	GATE/STILE
	MARSH
	SAND
	RIVER/STREAM

N

woodchips to produce a kipper which has a deserved reputation as the best in Britain.

Use the car park at the information centre, on the right as you enter the village by the only road. Walk down through the village, turn left at the harbour and follow the well sign-posted route to the castle. The walk is over springy turf above the shore line on a great shelf of whin which slopes up to landward. When the sea is running high, the force of the breakers on the shelving rocks can produce masses of creamy foam which often blows inland across the pasture.

Having visited the castle, regain the footpath by backtracking to the foot of the castle mound and follow the right of way through the low-lying area which once made the castle rock effectively an island. As the path crosses the fence beyond the castle take a look at the interesting rock formations on the beach. The most striking is a huge fold of strata which looks like an upturned boat, but students of geology will also find numerous dykes where volcanic rock has forced its way into faults.

From here the right of way goes straight up the golf links for about a mile and a quarter to the clubhouse. Those preferring not to run the gauntlet of flying golf balls can walk instead up the sandy beach of Embleton Bay, one of the prettiest on this, surely one of the best coastlines in all Britain.

At the clubhouse, on the left just after crossing Embleton Burn, our route cuts inland by the unmistakable road to Embleton village. Those taking the beach route should be sure to cut back to the clubhouse where the burn crosses the beach at a break in the dunes.

Alternatively, there is a rewarding two mile extension to the attractive village of Low Newton-by-the-Sea. Again the walk can be made either by the beach or – for those taking the golf course route – by continuing along the path past the clubhouse. Let us assume we are taking the beach route. The dunes on the left are higher and frequently dotted with little chalets. Low Newton itself is a mile along the beach and overlooks a vast sheltered natural harbour, a rare paradise for

~Bait diggers,
nr. Dunstanburgh~

JMA

windsurfers on this wild coast. There is a small shop and a pub, The Ship, which is little bigger.

To return, take the road behind the pub which dwindles eventually to a boardwalk through marshy dune land. There is a small tarn on the right a few hundred yards from the village where a wooden hide has been provided to watch the many species of wading and sea birds. The path continues, leading directly to the clubhouse to rejoin the original route.

On reaching Embleton village, turn left and fork left again after about 300 yards. After a similar distance the road turns sharp left by the wood. Take the signposted path across Embleton Burn at this corner.

The path soon reaches another wood which it skirts for a couple of hundred yards before dividing. Take the left fork through the wood and proceed direct for a mile until the road is joined. Follow the road, past Proctors Stead Farm (where occasional open days give the public an insight into farming) and take the left fork back towards Craster.

As the road makes a gentle sweep towards Craster, those with energy to spare can make another rewarding detour, this time of four miles, by taking the footpath which leaves the road at the outside of the bend.

At the edge of the wood beneath the escarpment, take the path to the right, following it across the field to the road at Craster South Farm. Cross the road and walk through the farmyard. The path then bears left, following a cart track, which dwindles to a path and eventually follows the edge of parkland surrounding Howick Hall. The hall (now only partly lived in) is worth a separate visit, and its extensive gardens contain numerous exotic shrubs.

The path emerges at the entrance to the grounds on a hairpin bend in the road. Turn left and follow the road half a mile to a sharp left bend. Continue here right and then left by a track to the shore. Follow the footpath to the right down to a sheltered cove at the far side of which is the Rumbling Kern, a rock formation which funnels the sea loudly through a natural sluice beneath a great arch.

Return to Craster by the path which follows the coast, except for short stretches where it reverts to the road because the former route by the cliff edge is deemed impassable.

The walk concludes by following the top of the dramatic whin cliffs at Cullernose Point, past the coastguard station and into Craster by the school.

Walk 4
CRAGSIDE HOUSE
NORTHUMBERLAND
10½ or 8½ miles

Once upon a time, Northumberland's rounded Cheviot Hills formed the heart of a huge volcano. Millions of years of erosion have left just the mountain's granite core. A few miles out from Cheviot itself, a chain of lower, sandstone hills forms a nearly complete ring and represents the remains of volcanic ashes thrown out long ago. The lower slopes of the Fell Sandstone ridge were often chosen as sites for country parks and mansions, their thin soils being suitable for tree planting but too poor for intensive grazing.

One such park was created in the 1860s by Lord Armstrong, arguably the most powerful of the Victorian industrialists and the founder of the huge Armstrong armaments works in Newcastle.

The unusual mansion was conceived as a fishing retreat and for entertaining important foreign clients. It contains many rooms in its rambling layout, about thirty being open to the public, furnished by the National Trust as authentically as possible. One houses the Trust's pre-Raphaelite de Morgan collection. Cragside is claimed to have been the first electrically lit house, courtesy of Sir Joseph Swan, the Tyneside inventor who, some claim, beat Edison in developing such illumination.

The stable block above Tumbleton Lake contains an interpretive centre and cafe. The house is usually open (except Monday) April to September, and in October on Wednesday, Saturday and Sunday. The surrounding

22

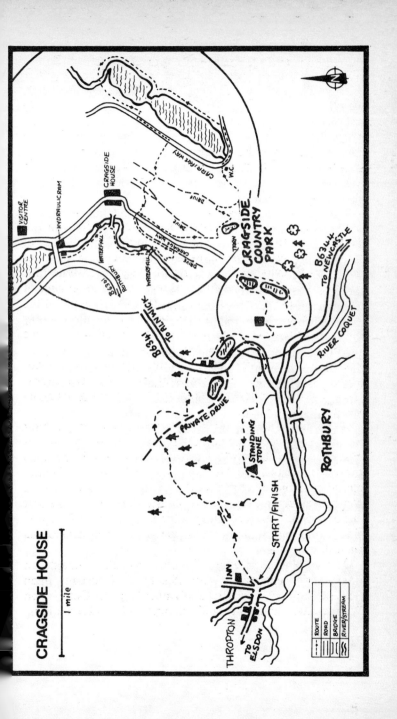

CRAGSIDE HOUSE

1 mile

country park is open daily in summer, but at weekends only in winter. It comprises 900 acres of craggy hillside in which Lord Armstrong created six lakes and tarns and planted many millions of trees, some possibly the tallest in Britain today.

Lord Armstrong was a great inventor in the field of hydraulics as well as munitions, and there are examples of his engineering in Debdon Gorge on the estate where rams raised water to the house and generators provided the power for Cragside's lighting. In the house, the lift and kitchen spit are also driven by water power.

The walker can get an idea of the Fell Sandstone range as it was before Cragside was built by making a three-mile moorland trek – sometimes steep – to the house and grounds.

The walk begins at Thropton, a village famed in the North-East for its curious variation of the pronunciation of the Northumbrian 'R'. One tale has it that this evolved through mimickry of the local laird who had a speech impediment. Thropton is on the B6341 in the Coquet valley west of the market town of Rothbury.

At the east end of the village, a public bridleway continues the lane on the right of the Cross Keys, climbing to over 800 feet to provide fine views across the valley to the rugged Simonside Hills, their lower slopes now – as with many of the Northumberland hills – in uniform Forestry Commission green. Approaching the cairn at the crest of the moor, the track forks. Taking the left branch, our walk circles woodland (go straight on at the crossroads at the edge of the woods) before dropping down to Debdon Burn. At the lodge, the drive passing Debdon Lake is closed off and it is necessary to double back slightly so as to reach the Rothbury to Alnwick road a little under two miles from the town.

Access to Cragside is by crossing the road. From here you can reach the visitor centre or strike away to the right after leaving the admission caravan, crossing the Debdon Burn at the head of Tumbleton Lake, and following the lakeside to the exit road.

Immediately below the exit road are the remains of Arm-

- Cragside Hall, Rothbury -

strong's hydraulics, beyond which the valley walk follows the right bank of the burn passing a waterfall and the iron bridge leading to the house. The bridge is closed for structural reasons, but from here you get the best view of the house, perched on the hillside.

The path can be followed down a narrow rocky gorge with another waterfall; below this, cross by the second small bridge to the far bank, and after a short distance zig-zag up to the Reiver's Well Drive; turn left to the house and forecourt which command a fine view over the iron bridge and the upper fall.

Those with an appetite for more walking (about two miles) after sampling the house can follow the terrace immediately on the left of the car road, joining the Crozier Drive to the tarn; this little rock-enclosed water is especially attractive at the beginning of the rhododendron season. From the near end of the tarn climb the hillside to Canada Drive, leading to the right in an arc to the high lakes on Nelly's Moss. Cross the lower dam to the right, following the road, then circle the two lakes anti-clockwise by a waterside path flanked first by pine woods and later by rhododendrons. Near the boathouse at the end of the dam which separates the lakes, turn up to the road and follow it to the left through the best of the shrub display, with views over flowers and the lower lake. Watch for a hidden footpath to the right, signposted to the house, which leaves the road about half-way along the lower lake; this crosses a plateau of exposed rock, heather and scrub before descending steeply to the forecourt.

To return to Thropton, pass from the forecourt through the archway under the house and leave the park by the main exit. After about half a mile to the left along the road to Rothbury, take the lane on the right to a line of houses set against the lower edge of the wood.

Here take the bridlepath to the right, up through the wood. After a short steep climb, the track forks and you should take the left branch which traverses first forest and then the moorland above Rothbury until the outward route is joined above Thropton.

Walk 5
KIELDERWATER
NORTHUMBERLAND
4 miles

In some ways Kielderwater is today a lasting reminder of the drought of 1976, for a by-product was the appointment of a 'Minister of Rain' and the notion of something akin to a national water grid. The building of a great new reservoir in the North Tyne valley acquired new political urgency. Today this great seven mile long lake – the largest man-made stretch of water in northern Europe, with four square miles – is connected by a complex series of tunnels linking the Pennine rivers with Teesside whose industrial decline has turned this costly exercise into something of a white elephant.

Whether the arrival of the great lake has improved the landscape is a matter for subjective judgement; there is no doubt it is slowly acquiring the beauty of a natural lake.

It should be remembered that the coming of the water is but the latest of many sweeping changes brought to this valley over the centuries. Fossilised trees in the peat are evidence of its heavily-wooded state before the landscape became largely heather moorland and bog, later used for shooting, as evidenced by the Dukes of Northumberland's shooting lodge at Kielder and that of the Swinburns at drowned Mounsey's Knowe.

In 1926 the Forestry Commission started an immense scheme for replanting nearly 200 square miles with conifers so that 50 years later this, the largest man-made forest in Europe, filled the upper valley and stretched over the hills into Redesdale and over the Scottish Border into Liddesdale.

27

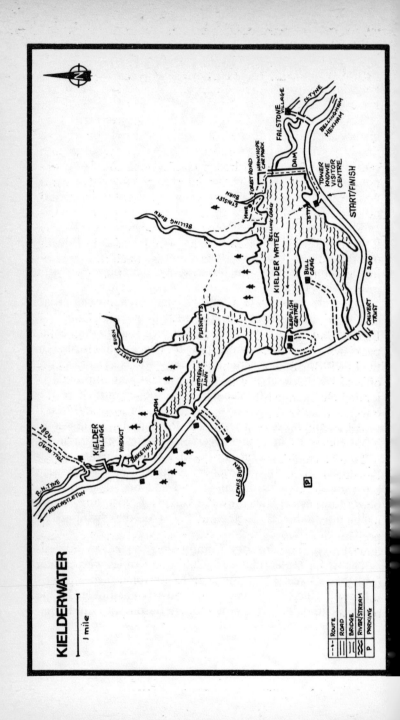

Before the timber was mature, the lower levels of the forest had to be felled to make way for the new arrival. At a narrow part of the valley above Falstone a three quarters of a mile long dam, 170 feet high, impounded 44 billion gallons of water 616 feet above sea level.

This was the greatest disturbance yet to an area with a long history of conflict. Once part of Scottish Strathclyde, it finally became English towards the end of the thirteenth century, though the border across the Debatable Land was not established until 1552. Not that peace followed, for this was the land of the Moss Troopers, the bands of Robsons and other families who raided the settlements of their rivals in Liddesdale and the richer lands further down the valleys. So it was a land of pele-towers, the fortified farms so numerous on both sides of the border. The only ancient church remaining, at Bellingham, has a possibly unique stone roof as a protection against fire.

There was mineral wealth in the valley – a four-foot-thick coal seam was readily drift-mined from the valleys of the Belling and Plashetts burns and the coal was carried by packhorse to the Scottish town of Newcastleton by tracks up the Lewis Burn and through the Cheviot passes. The promise offered by this industry led to the building of the railway joining Hexham to the Waverley Line from Carlisle to Edinburgh. Plashetts valley and much of the railway is now under water, and all that remains is the great viaduct over the River Tyne which was bought for preservation in 1969.

Tourist facilities followed the setting up in 1955 of the Northumberland National Park and the Border Forest Park, but the creation of Kielderwater has been the real take-off point for tourism since the Queen opened it in 1982. The name Kielder – derived from the Norse for spring – is perhaps appropriate, but the lake actually stretches away downstream from the forestry village of Kielder.

The many branch valleys have produced a very attractive irregular shape with a shoreline of 27 miles, so it is not suitable for a short circular walk! There are a number of car parks at the dam and along the southern shore, but as the

- Kelder Water -

north shore is the quiet, traffic-free side, we shall head for this, using the covered launches which operate in summer, and make the return journey on foot via the interesting feature of Belling Crag.

The Tower Knowe Visitor Centre is on a promontory jutting out into the south-east corner of the lake. Take the launch from here to the Plashetts landing to begin this walk along woodland paths and forest roads.

Leaving the launch, take the forest track inland and over the headland, maintaining the same direction at intersections until it begins to descend again. The direct route used to cross the now flooded valley of the Belling Burn, so you should bear left down into the valley.

After crossing the burn, fork right beside the ruined building, into the forest. Take the next right fork and then continue straight ahead for a little under a mile until a narrower track bears off right, signposted to Belling Crag. After a short distance take a footpath on the right which falls steeply through the woods (usually muddy); it is marked by a small sign which can easily be missed. The Belling was a knoll in the woods beside a small farm, now under water, and is now almost an island.

Where the path reaches the isthmus take the right-hand branch which takes you over the hill. This leads to the little crag on the water's edge which can be clearly seen from the Visitor Centre on the opposite shore. Continue eastwards round the headland and then by marked paths along the shore past the Staisley Burn bathing place to the Hawkhope car park. Alternatively, from the isthmus you can retrace your steps to the main track, thereby passing a small working drift mine buried in the forest which has survived the closing of the larger mines. Return to the car by the dam and the road.

Walk 6
ROMAN WALL
NORTHUMBERLAND
7 miles

The giant undertaking of the Emperor Hadrian in building a 75 mile wall at his northern frontier to keep out the marauding Picts has created a legacy which can truly be said to instil a flash of interest into Latin lessons at school. I well remember my own school visits to the Roman Wall – like many other schools and countless other daytrippers and holidaymakers we made for Housesteads Fort and the magnificent stretch of wall associated with it.

It is perhaps unfortunate that with 75 miles of wall to choose from, everyone should make for the same 12 mile stretch. But then with much of the rest either buried beneath the streets of Newcastle, plundered for later building work, or forming the foundation for the eighteenth-century Military Road – which spanned the country when invasion from the north remained an English preoccupation despite the Act of Union – neither is it surprising.

This most spectacular stretch of wall occurs where the terrain forced the line of the Military Road half a mile southward. The wall itself clings to the crest of a great length of crag formed by the Great Whin Sill – that intrusion of enormously tough volcanic rock which gives the North so many of its proudest features, from High Force to the castle mound at Dunstanburgh to Holy Island.

Housesteads Fort was built between 122AD and 130 as an exposed northerly garrison which must have seemed like pulling a very short straw to the 1,000 men posted there, even

A slate cairn that continues to grow as walkers add to it (*previous page*).

A gap in the clouds enlivens the view and makes the climb worthwhile (*above*).

Corries, formed by glaciers during the Ice Age, are a
feature of mountain areas (*right*).

High-level ridge walks are for those with a head for heights

Crags reflected in a mountain tarn (*right*).

**Lakes and moorland combine to produce the beautiful
and distinctive scenery of the Lake District.**

The north includes some of the remotest country in England (*right*).

A lake provides tranquility in contrast to the ruggedness of much of the surrounding scen

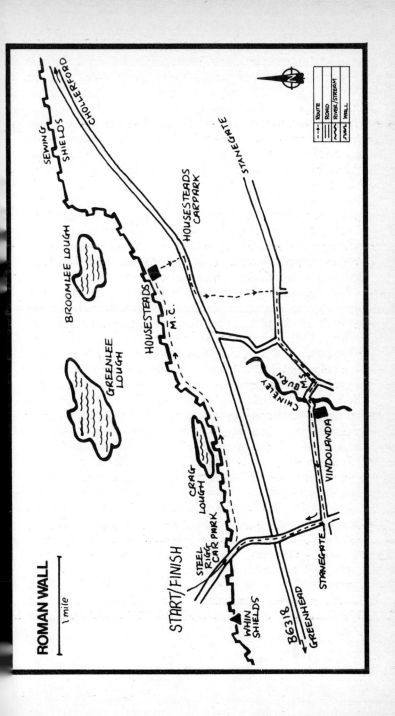

ROMAN WALL

1 mile

though research suggests the climate in Hadrian's time was a little less harsh than today. Housesteads Fort and museum are open daily except over the Christmas-New Year holiday, as are Vindolanda Fort and museum.

The landscape is so expansive it can absorb the number of visitors, but erosion to parts of the wall – which also carries the Pennine Way – is causing concern and walkers should take care to follow closely any new directions issued by those charged with conserving and restoring it.

The camp filled a five-acre rectangle sloping southward from the wall, heavily fortified and with massive double gates, later reduced in width. Within is the usual rectangular Roman street pattern and the ruins of the various civic and military buildings. On the larger terraced slope outside are the more haphazard relics of the settlement in which the civilian camp-followers collected.

The huge area from which Rome drew its legions is illustrated by the variety of gods to whom altars excavated were found to be dedicated: the extent is from northern Europe to Persia.

Our walk to Housesteads shuns the large car park half a mile below the fort and opts instead for the much smaller one at Steel Rigg, reached by turning north off the Military Road (B6318) at Twice Brewed at the crossroads by the pub.

The car park is adjacent to the wall about half a mile north of the Military Road. Half a mile to the west is Whinshields, the highest point on the wall at 1,121 feet, from where are fine views to Cross Fell, the Lake District and over the Solway Firth. This makes a worthwhile excursion before or after the main walk.

The latter takes us east, towards the distinctive Sewing-shields Crags, rich in Arthurian and other legends. After a slight dip comes the ascent of Steel Rigg and, after our first milecastle, the spectacular sheer face above Crag Lough.

The wall between milecastles was punctuated by turrets at intervals of a third of a mile, but the gaps in the Whin Sill, where the wall dips at intervals, are a reminder of its weakest aspect. In 1306 Edward based himself just south of Hotbank

Roman Wall — JHA

Pass to launch his last foray against the Scots.

Where the wall clings to the crest, the views north over the Northumbrian loughs to Kielder Forest and the Cheviots – which today mark the border with Scotland – are magnificent.

Beyond Hotbank Farm, from where the Pennine Way strikes off northward, is an easier climb to Hotbank Crags and Cuddy's Crags, another milecastle, then Housesteads, after a total of three miles of ridge.

By continuing along the wall a short distance beyond the fort you can visit the Knag Gate, inserted into the wall about 300AD as a frontier post and toll house on a civilian by-pass to Housesteads.

On reaching Housesteads, first call at the museum at the south-west corner to pay your admission charge and collect whatever informative brochures you need.

The return trip leaves Housesteads via the civilian settlement and the main car park. Follow the Military Road west for about half a mile before taking the bridleway on the left which leads, after three quarters of a mile, to Stanegate, the Roman road which runs between the wall and the River Tyne. On reaching the road, turn right and descend to the Roman fort at Vindolanda, which involves a well-signed right turn after about a mile.

The circuit is completed by continuing along Stanegate another mile to a crossroads where a right turn will bring you back to Once Brewed and Steel Rigg.

Walk 7
GIBSIDE CHAPEL
TYNE & WEAR/CO DURHAM
5½ miles

New York's Statue of Liberty stands defiantly proclaiming the ideals of a nation to the world. By contrast, she has a British namesake which stands lonely and inaccessible in a secluded country estate. Remarkably, the statue tops a 140 feet column – higher than Nelson's – and is just a few miles from the banks of the Tyne at its most industrial. But it stands on private land belonging to the Earls of Strathmore and visitors must content themselves with admiring it across a wooded gorge from the end of a magnificent avenue lined with exotic Turkey oaks. However, there is no such restriction applying to the unusual Gibside Chapel, built at the other end of the avenue in the style of a Greek temple by James Paine (who was probably also responsible for the statue) in the late eighteenth century. The chapel, with its imposing Ionic portico and cruciform plan crowned with a low dome, was presented to the National Trust in 1965, along with the avenue. Inside are unusual box pews and a three-deck pulpit, while the Bowes family mausoleum is below.

Gibside Chapel is open daily except Tuesdays, April to September; Wednesdays and weekends, October and March, and Sundays only November to February. Admission is free.

The landscaped park was created by Sir George Bowes in the eighteenth century when the land came into the family by marriage. Sir George also had Gibside Hall enlarged: today, its ruined shell and that of the Orangery stand on the

GIBSIDE CHAPEL

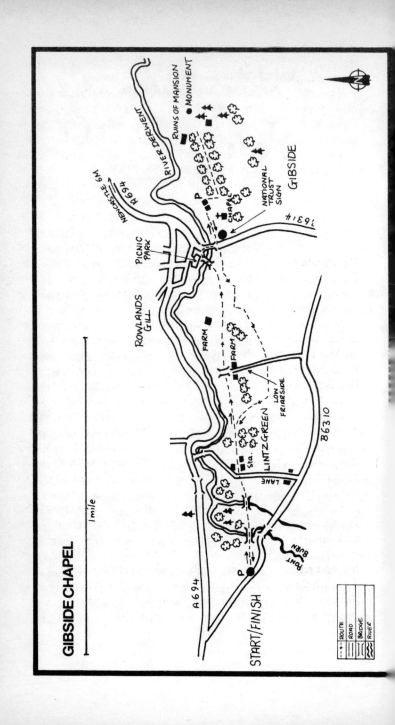

1 mile

ROUTE
ROAD
BRIDGE
RIVER

START/FINISH

A 694

PONT BURN

P

LINTZ GREEN

LANE

Sta.

B 6310

LOW FRIARSIDE

FARM

FARM

ROWLANDS GILL

PICNIC PARK

NEWCASTLE 6M

R 694

RIVER DERWENT

RUINS OF MANSION

MONUMENT

CHAPEL

P

NATIONAL TRUST SIGN

1631 H

GIBSIDE

N

escarpment on the north side of the avenue. The chapel is said to be a favourite of the Queen Mother because of its connection with her Bowes ancestors.

The walk to Gibside follows the old Derwent Valley Railway, whose tracks were lifted in 1962 after almost 100 years. Reasons for the line's downfall lay in the fact that it rarely passed close to the centre of the communities it was supposed to serve, as the engineers strove to find the best route along the valley side towards Consett.

The result of the engineers' endeavours was a number of admirable structures in the best tradition of Victorian railway architecture, the legacy of which is a beautifully secluded and at times spectacular walk. The main engineering feats were the excavation of a half mile long 60 foot deep cutting north of Rowlands Gill and the construction of four large viaducts. Durham County Council reclaimed the line, renovated it and opened it in 1972 as a ten-mile footpath, bridleway and cycle track stretching from Gateshead almost to Consett.

There are several well-signposted points of access to the track, with parking for cars. The most beautiful and spectacular stretch of about two and a half miles is that starting from High Hamsterley on the B6310, near its junction with the A694 Gateshead to Consett road. There are frequent buses from Newcastle and Consett along the A694 to its junction with the B6310 at the far end of the Hamsterley Mill estate, about half a mile from the starting point.

A short slope brings the walker to the shrub and tree-edged track stretching, it seems, to infinity. There is no break in the greenery until the stone parapets of the first viaduct appear in the distance.

This is 600 feet long and about 120 feet high as it spans the Pont Burn, almost invisible below. In every direction, trees and nothing but trees feast the eyes. Far below, their tops bend in the wind, and there is a feeling of being cut off from life and reality. In spring or autumn the colours are superb. The whole area is rich in animal and birdlife, and wild flowers. Watch for deer, foxes and – if you are lucky and choose your time – badgers.

– Gibside Chapel –

View from the
Gibside Chapel

Moving on through arches of willow and alder, the way clears again at the second viaduct, 90 feet high, before Lintz Green Station, a full quarter of a mile from the tiny community which gave it its name. Here remain a platform, a few railway houses, and a flight of steps up to the station master's house and the narrow access road. Although isolated, the houses are all occupied.

Returning to the track: on the left, falling down to the Derwent, are cultivated fields. Further on, to the west of the line, a ruined chapel stands in a field. It is said to have been founded about 1150 by a hermit named John. The building was enlarged in the thirteenth century but in 1539 Henry VIII pensioned off the chaplain at £5 per year and had the bell removed from the tower.

After crossing the third viaduct, over the Derwent itself, to Rowlands Gill Country Park picnic area, a right turn brings the walker down to the road bridge on the B6314 from where a short walk uphill leads to Gibside Chapel and mausoleum.

To return to Hamsterley, cross the B6314 to the farm road almost opposite. From this the railway walk can be reached without crossing the river. Alternatively, where the path rejoins the railway track, you can bear left, sticking to the path through the woods (conditions underfoot permitting) and rejoin the railway a mile further west between Low Friarside and Lintz Green. This route takes the walker up the valley side, from which elevation the line chosen by the railway engineers can be well appreciated.

This walk combines well with a car trip to nearby Beamish open-air industrial museum or with a ride on the restored Tanfield railway.

Walk 8
PENSHAW MONUMENT
TYNE & WEAR
7½ miles

From miles around, Penshaw Monument can be seen standing like a northern Parthenon on its hill overlooking Washington New Town – indeed, its great Doric pillars are visible throughout much of what was once the county of Tyne and Wear. It is a folly in the finest style, saved from an undignified crumbling fate by the National Trust.

The roofless temple is 100 feet long, 53 feet wide and 70 feet high, with 28 columns. It was built as a double-size replica of the Temple of Theseus in the 1840s by public subscription as a tribute to John George Lambton, the First Earl of Durham. 'Radical Jack' was a descendant of an earlier Lambton whose carelessness, legend has it, bred a fearsome serpent which he eventually had to slay on his return from the Crusades. There is open access to the monument.

Washington's name gives a clue to historic connections which place it firmly on the itinerary of Americans 'doing Britain'. The Old Hall, a restored manor house now in the hands of the National Trust, was the seat of George Washington's family with its stars and stripes coat of arms.

The walk to Penshaw Monument takes you from the National Trust Wildfowl Park via the attractive wooded valley which links them.

There is a car park beside the reserve and this is reached by taking the A195 Washington turn-off on the A1M at Birtley services and following the Sunderland signs. There is a slip road for the park a short distance after leaving the new town,

PENSHAW MONUMENT

1 mile

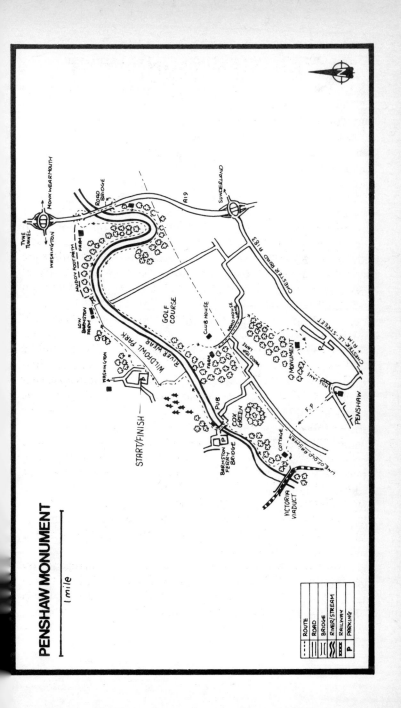

and a little more than a mile short of the junction with the A19 (from which direction it can also be approached).

In addition to native and migrating wild birds – of which nearly 100 kinds have been observed – there are some 1,200 residents representing more than 100 species from all over the world. There is a fine log cabin visitor centre with an excellent viewing room and other facilities. The park is open daily except Christmas and Boxing Days. There are buses from Newcastle, Sunderland or Chester-le-Street (not Sunday).

Leave the car park by the exit road and turn right along the cinder track (signposted to Low Barmston, and probably muddy!). At next sign (to North Hylton), turn off right over the footbridge and follow the wildfowl park perimeter fence, finally zig-zagging down steps towards the riverside. The path is now a good chipped surface but with numerous steps.

At a second, larger footbridge over a stream, the path forks – the left-hand path leads direct over fields to the A19 bridge over the Wear. It is uninteresting and very muddy, so it is worth taking the longer woodland path by the riverside where you will find a fine display of celandines in spring.

Approaching the road bridge, the path climbs gradually to its level. Ignoring signs which can be rotated by idle hands, bear left into the farm and then right beyond the new-looking house. After passing under the A19 take the steps up to it and cross the bridge, leaving it on the far bank by the path which swings round and passes under it to reach the south bank of the Wear, which can now be followed through woods to the golf course.

Keep to the river bank for a further one and a half miles and re-enter woods. After 200 yards turn left up the Copperas Gill past the golf club house to reach Woodhouse Lane by the old railway track. Go straight ahead, not right to Cox Green, continuing for about 200 yards to where a path on the right leads uphill to the corner of Penshaw Hill wood. Turn right again and follow the southern edge of the wood to the monument. Please use the stiles!

Note that the old railway track can be used as a short cut

— Penshaw Monument —

from the A19 where it can be joined by staying on the A19 a little further before crossing beneath it by a second bridge.

On a clear day the monument offers a clear view across Tyneside and Wearside and you can reflect on once prosperous times represented by distant shipyard cranes, or on what some see as the dawning of a new industrial era for the North-East, as symbolised by the clean square lines of the Nissan plant.

Head left along the edge of the wood down the slope westward towards Penshaw church. Penshaw means 'wooded hill', and was an ancient oak wood until the seventeenth century. On reaching the main street at the foot of Hill Lane turn right and then follow the field path down the hill. Cross the lower Cox Green by-road and abandoned railway at right angles (footpath sign To Wear), to a cottage near the end of the Victoria Viaduct.

This fine structure, with four main spans, was completed

45

on the day of Victoria's coronation to carry the original London-Newcastle main line, but is now used only by diverted services. It is 128 feet above the river and its arches were then claimed to be the largest in Europe.

Pass in front of the cottage (beware dogs and goats), swing left and then follow the woodland path down to the right. Turn right on the main valley path, downriver, though you will at first be separated from the river by the site of some old staithes – landing stages. On the right of the path you can see the tunnels by which stone was brought to the staithes for loading on to 'keels'. The riverside wood is natural mixed deciduous. Just past the first houses of Cox Green you will see Alice's Well, until recently the only water supply. The Oddfellows Arms, just past the bridge, serves bar snacks. Cross the Wear by the footbridge which has now replaced the ferry.

From the car park on your left the James Steel Country Park follows the tributary river to Washington town centre, but you turn right behind the first house and follow the signposted path to the Wildfowl Park, just above the river, and then up to the perimeter fence of the refuge.

Walk 9
DURHAM CATHEDRAL
DURHAM
3 miles

So many writers have heaped adulation on Durham that it is hard to find new superlatives to describe this city which, once seen, has to be visited and revisited to be explored and enjoyed to the full.

Back in the early eighteenth century, long before modern trends in travel and tourism, Daniel Defoe described 'the magnificence and splendour' in which lived the bishop and the clergy, perched in their fine houses on the wooded sandstone promontory which is all but enclosed by a loop in the River Wear.

But dominating them all is Durham Cathedral, voted the world's finest building by 300 of Britain's 'top people' in a 1984 survey to mark the start of a National Festival of Architecture. Not everyone would agree with the judges in putting the cathedral ahead of the Parthenon or the Taj Mahal, but there can be no disputing its claim as the finest example of Norman architecture in Britain, if not Europe.

Durham's first church was a shrine for the body of St Cuthbert, of Lindisfarne, built in 995; work on the present cathedral began in 1093. The building of the castle which encloses it began in 1070 as a defence against the Scots and it was under the rule of a prince bishop appointed by the king – the prince bishops ruled until 1836 with complete authority over a kingdom which stretched north to the Tweed.

In 1833, the last prince bishop, Van Mildert, gave up his use of the castle and endowed it to found Durham University

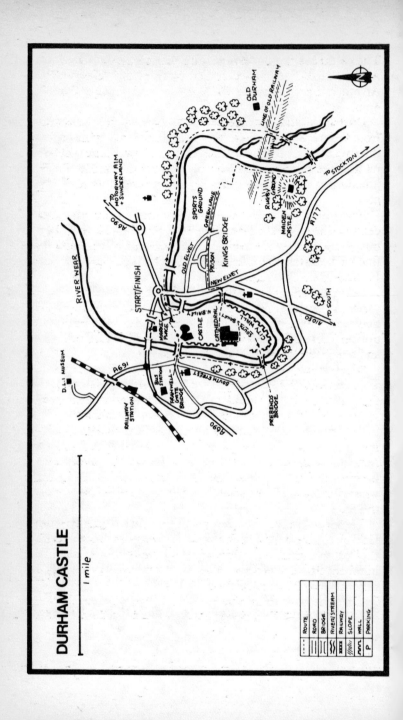

when Parliament made it the third university in England. The castle is open on Wednesdays during the first week of April and from July to September, mornings and afternoons. At other times, Monday, Wednesday and Friday, 2pm – 4pm.

Durham is usually approached by road along the A690 from the A1(M). As it descends from the motorway towards the river, this gives a gradually emerging view of the cathedral and the castle. At the second roundabout (at the A177 junction) take the second exit leading to a multi-storey car park.

From here the walk takes you first away from the city centre via the attractive gorge of the Wear. Those arriving by bus, or by train to the station at its lofty vantage at the end of a fine viaduct above the west of the city, can join the walk at Framwellgate Bridge, as shown on the map.

Leave the car park by the bottom exit and walk the few yards to the riverside where you can get snacks at the boathouse, take a river cruise or hire a boat, in season. Turn left, upriver, beneath the gardens of St Hild's and Bede colleges and along the pleasantly wooded riverbank.

Where the woods leave the water's edge, take the path which crosses the field (often very wet), cross the old railway, then take the stile and head across the field for the pedestrian suspension bridge across the river to the sports field.

Cross the river and turn right along the bank, back towards the city. Above you, on your left, is the wooded hill of Maiden Castle, once a fort. Continue along the riverbank, keeping the rugby ground on your left. Keep to the path where it leaves the river to reach Green Lane; take this lane to the left.

The open parkland on the right is the site of the Miners' Gala on the third Saturday in June, though the contraction of the coal mining industry has caused a steady decline in the numbers attending the gala, which is bedecked by the magnificent banners of all the county's pits.

Continue on the now-metalled road – the high wall looming on your left is Durham Prison. Bear left across the front

49

Durham

of the prison and cross New Elvet to Dunelm House, the students' union building. Here a path and steps lead to the modern footbridge over the river designed by the architect Ove Arap. Pause a minute on the bridge to look downstream (left) and admire the thickly wooded river banks which are at their most magnificent in autumn.

Continue straight up Bow Lane to Palace Green where the houses, hospitals and almhouses which surround it date back to the fifteenth century; all are now occupied by the university. The cathedral is straight ahead: look for the large Dun Cow carved on this, the north face – legend has it the animal played a part leading the Lindisfarne monks to this final resting place for St Cuthbert's body.

Unusually, Durham Cathedral has no west door and entry is by the North Door with its famous sanctuary knocker. Go to the west end of the cathedral, the Galilee Lady Chapel, where the Venerable Bede is buried and look out of the small window straight down the precipice to the river. On a clear day, summon your energy and climb the tower for a magnificent view across the city and beyond.

Exit and turn left and left again to a small memorial garden where you can sit and admire more attractive old houses across College Green, occupied by clergy attached to the cathedral.

Leaving the garden, turn left to the Priors' Archway and right along the South Bailey – the houses here are now departments or colleges of the university. Have a look at the interesting door knockers and fanlights. Descend through the city wall to cross Prebends' Bridge from which there is a superb view of the cathedral.

Walk along the riverbank to your right to Framwellgate Bridge and climb the steps to cross the river into Silver Street leading to Market Place.

Explore the covered market and the Guildhall, then leave the Market Place by Saddler Street and fork left down a pedestrian street towards Old Elvet bridge, descending the steps on your left before crossing the bridge and returning via the boathouse to the car park.

Walk 10
KILLHOPE WHEEL
NORTHUMBERLAND & CO DURHAM
8 miles

Some of the least visited Pennine dales are those which radiate from the high ground where Northumberland, Durham and Cumbria meet. This high region is the birthplace of the three great North-East rivers – Tyne, Wear and Tees – and of the Nent and the two Allens which flow into the South Tyne.

Tight, winding valleys cut back into hills bare of all but heather and coarse grass, home only of curlew, lapwing, grouse and a few sheep. Roads are confined to the valley bottoms with a few high passes which remain blocked or treacherous through most winter months. The lower hillsides are dotted with numerous stone cottages, small farms, barns – many abandoned and ruined – linked by a tangle of lanes and paths.

This was a centre of the lead industry for many centuries, probably since Roman times, reaching its prime in the eighteenth and the first half of the nineteenth centuries. Mining in Australia and America in the latter half brought prices crashing, and British mining was no longer profitable. Sheep raising on small farms combined with knitting and work in the mines to support families, giving rise to the scattering of buildings outside the main settlements.

Near the head of the Killhope Burn, a tributary of the Wear, stands one of the few remaining monuments to the lead industry – Killhope Wheel. The only other survivors are the remains of some of the great flues which climbed the

KILLHOPE WHEEL

1 mile

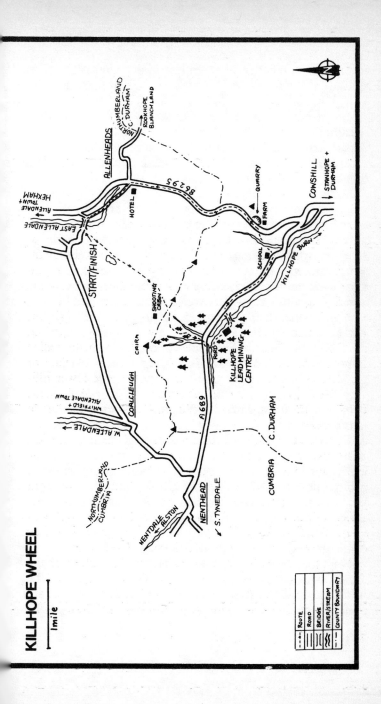

····	ROUTE
‖‖‖	ROAD
⋈	BRIDGE
≈≈	RIVER/STREAM
—·—	COUNTY BOUNDARY

START/FINISH

ALLENHEADS

ALLENDALE TOWN + HEXHAM

EAST ALLENDALE

HOTEL

B6295

NORTHUMBERLAND / C. DURHAM

ROOKHOPE BLANCHLAND

QUARRY

FARM

SCHOOL

KILLHOPE BURN

COWSHILL

STANHOPE + DURHAM

SHOOTING CABIN

CAIRN

COALCLEUGH

WHITFIELD + ALLENDALE TOWN

W. ALLENDALE

A689

FORD

KILLHOPE LEAD MINING CENTRE

CUMBRIA   C. DURHAM

NORTHUMBERLAND CUMBRIA

NENTDALE   ALSTON

NENTHEAD

S. TYNEDALE

hillsides from the smelting furnaces to great moortop chimneys. Hidden underground are hundreds of workings, mainly small, though one underground drainage canal was large enough for barges to carry early tourists for many miles.

At Killhope, the buildings which served the Park Level Mine are being preserved, and, where necessary, restored, using stone and timber from the adjacent forest and metal worked in the original forge. The huge iron waterwheel is the key feature and has been a local landmark for 125 years. More than 40 feet in diameter, it was the largest of those working the plant and survived when other parts became decayed and buried. The channels and flumes which brought the water are being restored and at the time of writing it was expected the wheel would be turning again by 1988.

Visitors should start their inspection at the 'Shop', where men and boys spent the weekday nights rather than walking to and from their homes if these were distant. Crowded four or five to a bunk, they derived a little warmth and comfort not only from their cooking fire but also from the smithy and stables below.

The rooms also hold samples of ore, tools, lead products and working models with recorded commmentaries. Other buildings on the site are the bousteads, where the ore worked by the various groups of miners was separately stored for sorting and for despatch to the crusher, and to the jaggers, trommels and buddles by which lead and waste were separated. The Wheel buildings are open daily from April to October.

The approach walk is tougher than those described at lower altitudes, being between 1,200 and 2,100 feet. Warm clothes, stout boots, a compass and the ability to use it, are recommended. Though there are no dangerous precipices, these hills are exposed, and snow may lie in the gullies past mid-summer. The rough grass and heather make for heavy going, for there are no longer miners to keep the tracks worn and clear on their way to work.

The suggested starting place is at the foot of Stag Hill, about one and a quarter miles north-west of Allenheads near

Killhope Mine Centre

Dirt Pot hostel. Follow the cart track (which starts at the west end of the bridge and is signposted to Coalcleugh) south-west for a mile-and-a-half until it veers away to the right to a shooting cabin high up Killhope Law.

Here you should leave the track, continuing on a south-west bearing to cross the ridge, a little under a mile to the east of the Law (distinguishable by a large cairn). The ridge is crossed about two-thirds of the way across a shallow col. Continuing on the same bearing as you descend will keep you a quarter of a mile to the left of the nearer of two small plantations on your right and will lead you to the right-hand corner of a large wood.

A fence round the head of the valley to the right of the wood will ensure you do not get lost among cliffs and water-falls. Enter the wood by the stile and gate and follow the well-cleared ride down to meet the A689 Durham-Alston road opposite the Killhope picnic site. The ford may be avoided by using the bridge downstream.

For the return journey from Killhope Wheel, follow the main road for one and a half miles down the valley. It is highly unlikely that much traffic will be encountered, but remember to walk on the right.

After passing the old school on your left, turn left up the signed footpath, cross a small stream and head for the quarry just left of High Greenfield farm house, which is in view all the way. Join the B6295, follow it to the left (across the county boundary) and down into Allenheads. Turn left, pass the hotel and continue down the by-road to the starting point. Extensive abandoned lead workings can be seen on the other bank.

This is an ideal route for a double party in which some members walk across the moor while the car is taken over the high moorland road through Coalcleugh at the head of the West Allen to the outskirts of Nenthead and left down to the Killhope Wheel. An exchange of drivers will enable the rest of the party to enjoy the return walk over the ridge.

Walk 11
LONG MEG
CUMBRIA
5 miles

The quiet pastoral land of the Eden Valley, cradled between the mountains of the Lakes and the highest part of the
Pennine range, is especially enjoyed by discerning visitors
who prefer peace and solitude to full-to-bursting bar-rooms,
garish gift shops and cars, cars, cars.

This walk gives a taste of many things typical of the valley:
the sandstone cliffs, the little villages, the railway architecture. Our goal is Long Meg and her Daughters – a druid
monolith and stone circle claimed by some to be the second
largest neolithic circle in the country after Stonehenge and
whose origin is put at about 4,500BC.

The suggested starting point is at Little Salkeld which is
reached by turning north off the A686 Penrith to Alston road
and driving for a mile and a half. Ignore the first sign an-
nouncing your arrival at the village and continue, crossing
beneath the railway and bearing left.

Entering Little Salkeld you will see the restored water mill
on your right. Continue up the hill to the T-junction and turn
left, passing the grounds of the Hall on your left down a
narrow lane marked as a no through road. After a couple of
hundred yards the road forks and further vehicle access is
restricted. Take the left fork and park carefully on the verge.
The footpath follows the other fork and is signposted Lacy
Caves and Dale Raven.

Little Salkeld can also be reached by catching the train
from Carlisle or Skipton to Langwathby and walking from

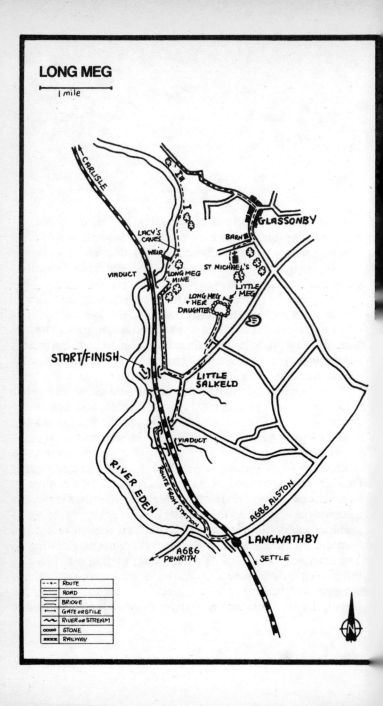

LONG MEG

|⊢———————⊣|
1 mile

there, though this spectacular line is under a long-standing closure threat.

Follow the concrete and tarmacadam road, keeping the railway on your left, passing after three quarters of a mile a derelict winding and engine house built about 1880. The track here descends to the right, apparently leaving the railway as it enters woodland. Soon you are confronted by prominent notices advising you to keep out of Long Meg. This refers not to the stone circle but to the former British Gypsum mine which closed in 1973 after about 100 years.

Take the well-signposted detour to the left, dog-legging past the large electricity sub-station, then following the path to the right to where it has been realigned to follow the railway alongside what used to be the sidings for this once busy generator of rail freight.

As the path leaves the railway to join the river bank in thick woodland, note the seven-arch viaduct built in typical Midland Railway style of locally quarried red sandstone to stand in harmony with its surroundings.

The path continues through pine and rhododendron, its fringes blue with harebells in spring. Note the occasional remnants of an old mineral line which ends at the site of an early mine and a brickworks. The Eden is met quite high above Force Weir, which the big river crosses with some commotion. Here was one of the earliest crossings of the Eden, to Force Knott Castle on the left bank. The bridge was washed away several times, the last being early this century.

Follow the river bank path a short distance further by the old miners' track and you reach the remarkable Lacy Caves and a rather forbidding sign which reads: 'This path is dangerous – proceed at your own risk, by permission of the landowner'. In fact, although the caves are hewn out of a sheer sandstone promontory above the Eden, there is no danger provided reasonable care is taken, particularly in wet weather.

The caves were carved out of the red rock in the eighteenth century on the instructions of Lt Col Samuel Lacy of Salkeld Hall. Local historian Alan Earnshaw suggests that they

~Long Meg~

comprised a wine cellar and summer house along the lines of those seen by Lacy on his travels to Gibraltar and elsewhere.

Rejoin the path by back-tracking and taking the new steps up and over the promontory. Note the beech, oak and Norwegian spruce, planted by Lacy in line with fashion. The path soon issues into a more open area where it winds among newly-planted conifers, harebells and campion.

At the end of the wood enter the meadow by the stile, and immediately cross a second stile on your left. The path is poorly defined here, but the correct route is to stick parallel with the river. At the end of the meadow, cross the stile and descend the steps through the wood to the road. The road is then followed to the right as far as Glassonby, with a fine view of Cross Fell ahead.

Bear right through Glassonby, passing a substantial manor-style farmhouse on your right; note the 1604 date stone above the door of the adjacent Home Farm. A couple of hundred yards further, take the lane on the right at the two barns.

Now you are confronted not by Pennine peaks but those of Lakeland as you head for the small church on your left. This is St Michael's, the parish church of Addingham, a village on the banks of the Eden which was washed away when the river burst its banks and changed course in 1350. Walk through the well-kept churchyard, noting some very early tombstones and the four-holed hammer-head cross outside the porch. Exit by the gate in the far wall and walk straight down the track through the conifer nursery.

Cross the lane and enter the next field by the gate which is marked with a yellow arrow on a green background. Keep to the right-hand edge of the field until you come to a stile beside a young conifer thicket, again marked by a yellow arrow. Follow the marked route, bearing right.

Continue heading slightly left of the farm in the distance, by way of another stile, coming eventually into a field where a strangled oak stands over to the right. Follow the hedge up the left of the field and cross the stile to bring you to the stone circle.

It is said that if you walk round the circle counting the stones, you will never come to the same number twice – but if you did the witch Long Meg would come to life or the Devil would appear!

To return to Little Salkeld, follow the metalled road which cuts through the corner of the stone circle. Continue down the unmade track where the road turns sharp left and join the road just above the village.

Walk 12
BOWES MUSEUM
CO. DURHAM
9 or 7 miles

The bleak trans-Pennine pass over Stainmore has been of great strategic importance throughout history. The Romans built a road across it, linking a line of forts and signal stations, while at the eastern end their Brigantean enemies built their great fortified stronghold of Stanwick. Later the Normans replaced the Roman forts at Brough and Bowes with their characteristic castles, but these were only two of the numerous castles and towers which defended their area.

About 1150, Bernard Balliol rebuilt a castle erected by his father after the Conquest, and the town which grew up under its protection took the name of Barnard Castle. It is a pleasant grey-stone market town, largely eighteenth century. The castle is hidden from the streets, but viewed across the river it towers dramatically from a near vertical cliff above the elegant Elizabethan bridge over the Tees.

At the lip of the escarpment, the Market Place is almost separated from The Bank at the end of Newgate by a most attractive colonnaded butter market crowned by an octagonal town hall and cupola of Palladian design.

Barnard Castle's jewel, however, is the Bowes Museum, on Newgate. This huge building in the style of a French chateau was designed in the 1860s by a French architect for George Bowes of Streatlam Castle, a few miles to the north (demolished in 1927), and his French wife. Bowes was another member of that famous family which came over with the Conqueror to build Bowes Castle, defend Barnard Castle

62

BOWES MUSEUM

1 mile

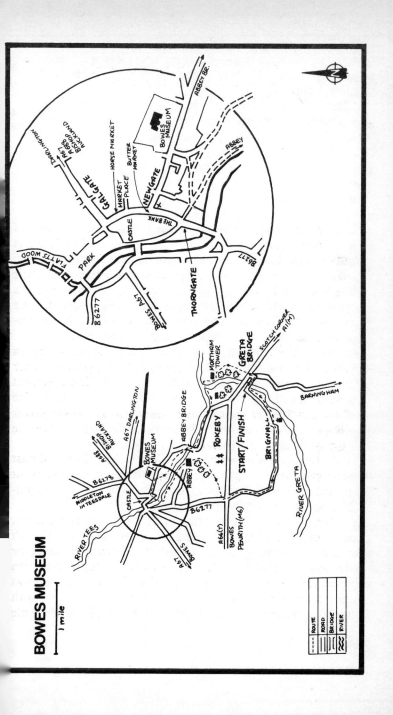

during the sixteenth-century Rising of the North, rebuild Streatlam as a huge mansion, inherit Gibside (the objective of another walk in this book) and found the maternal line of the Queen's ancestry.

The museum was set up in 20 acres of grounds to house the huge family collection of continental art but the endowment proved inadequate and it is now administered by Durham County Council. It has everything from Roman antiquities to period rooms, but is particularly rich in French furniture and art. Open daily except Christmas week, New Year's Day and Sunday mornings.

Also of interest are the nineteenth-century restoration of a Norman church remodelled by Richard III, in Newgate, the oldest of the town houses, Blagraves House at the head of the Bank, and the King's Head Hotel where Dickens researched Nicholas Nickleby and was inspired to write Master Humphrey's Clock.

Our walk joins the museum and town to the valley of the Greta, recorded in many paintings by Turner and Cotman, and the inspiration of Walter Scott and the poet Robert Southey. The eighteenth-century Greta Bridge has now been by-passed by the A66, and the loop of old road by the Morritt Arms Hotel, survivor of three former coaching inns, makes a convenient parking-place.

Leave the road at the east end of the hump-backed bridge by the stile in the wall on the left, passing under the by-pass to the wooded knoll which marks the eastern extremity of Rokeby Park, the Morritt's Palladian mansion. Keep the wall on your left to the field gate, carry on across the field by the ash trees to the barn.

Straight on, the path reaches the end of a lane leading past Mortham Tower to the mouth of the Greta at the Meeting of the Waters. The tower is the fourteenth-century fortified house of the Rokebys, now shorn of the Tudor wings which surrounded the courtyard.

Cross the Greta by the Dairy Bridge, having a look at the rocky pools and miniature cliffs, go through the wicket gate and follow the south bank of the Tees to the Abbey Bridge

— Barnard Castle —

and cross to the woodland footpath on the far bank.

Thanks to replanting this may be very muddy, in which case follow the road up the hill for a quarter of a mile to a bend and seat; from there a second footpath follows higher ground. Both footpaths lead to the Demesne Fields, from the right-hand side of which Parson's Lonnen leads to the museum (entrance to your right).

After visiting the museum, turn right to enter the town by Newgate. After the butter cross, the entrance to the castle is at the right-angled bend in the main street at the junction of Horse Market and Galgate. The King's Head Hotel is in front of you and the church on your left.

Leave the town centre down The Bank, past the cross and Blagraves House on your left; continue down Thorngate and across the footbridge.

Follow the riverside path to the twelfth-century Egglestone Abbey, set in a magnificent position above the steep

65

river bank. Although roofless, most of the walls of the great cruciform church are standing, complete with the early English tracery of the windows. After the Dissolution the monastic buildings were converted into a manor house, also now in ruins.

Leave the abbey car park by the farm road and turn left through the farmyard. Beyond the gate turn left over the stream bridge and then alongside the small stream, keeping parallel with a long straight wood 100 yards to your right. Level with a wood on your left, turn right to the first wood and follow its edge round to the right; at its corner, strike diagonally left as shown on the map, heading for the farm two fields away at Cross Lanes on the B6277.

Cross the A66 (with care) to the Brignall by-road; follow this, bearing left through the roadside plantation. At Brignall village take the footpath on the right of the church to reach the wooded bank of the Greta and follow this back to Greta Bridge.

The walk can be reduced to seven miles by omitting the famous Brignall Bank and returning to the car from Egglestone Abbey by the by-road, keeping the wall of Rokeby Hall on your left.

Walk 13
STAITHES HARBOUR
CLEVELAND & NORTH YORKSHIRE
7½ miles

The people of Teesside in search of fresh air and exercise are almost certain to strike out south to the spectacular escarpment of the North York Moors, or east along the equally spectacular coastline formed where the same escarpment meets the sea.

Of the little harbours in the cliffs, probably the most spectacular is Staithes, sheltering beneath a sheer cliff, Cowbar Nab, at the eastern end of the 666 foot high Boulby cliffs. The beck at the edge of the village forms the North Yorkshire boundary and although Staithes is technically a few yards outside the province of this book, it is nonetheless historically linked with the North-East and a rewarding goal for a walk which straddles the new – and typically ill-conceived – county boundary.

Once a haunt of smugglers, it became an important fishing port. Staithes' most famous inhabitant was James Cook, apprenticed to a grocer here. The harbour is vulnerable and the grocer's shop was swept away in 1740; the Cod and Lobster pub suffered that fate three times. There were other excitements, including a naval invasion by the American privateer Paul Jones at the end of the 18th century.

The old part of Staithes at the foot of a narrow cleft in the cliffs is a place for walking. No parking is allowed in the narrow streets and virtually none at the harbour.

There is space for parking near Roxby Church two miles inland, approached most easily by the road leading from the

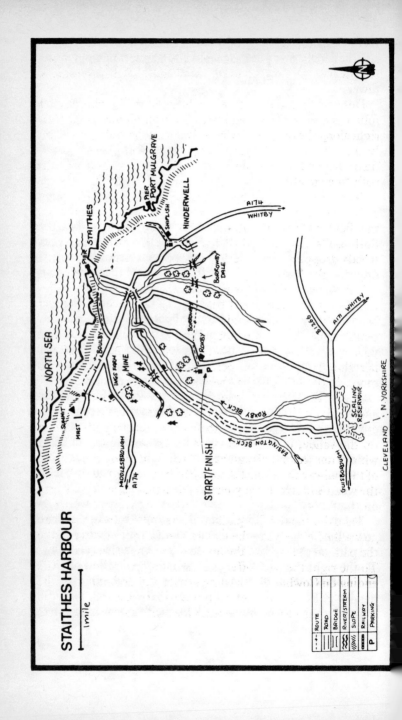

A171 Guisborough-Whitby road at Scaling Reservoir, opposite the picnic site. After one and a half miles the road drops steeply past the Fox Inn to the small church with a landmark tower.

Descend the sunken lane on the right of the church and follow the edge of the field with the wall on your left; turn right along the top of the woods which fill the valley of Roxby Beck. After about 300 yards cross the stile in a corner of the field; descend the shoulder of the hill by a steep woodland path to a small bridge.

Just beyond the bridge take the left-hand path, which strikes up the hillside to a stile at the edge of the wood; cross the field by an ancient hedge to Ridge Hall. Cross the Scaling-Dalehouse road (a beautiful road southwards with woods dropping away steeply from both margins) to a stile opposite the farm.

Take a bearing on Ings Farm, across the valley of Easington Beck with a high mast behind it. This is what you must head for during the next mile or so. To the right is the Boulby potash mine, seen, unfortunately, at its clearest. Try to close your eyes to it and remember that it is the major employer hereabouts now that 90 per cent of the fishing fleet is no more. It is, at 4,000 feet the country's deepest mine.

Across the field a stile leads into the next wooded valley and the path drops very steeply through thick trees. After crossing the stream, ease to the right to meet a path coming up the valley, turning left up it to the wood edge, beyond which runs the mine's railway. Turn right along the far side of the railway for a short distance to bear left up the hill with the wood and stream on your left, bringing you to Ings Farm on the A174.

Take the sunken footpath on the left of the farm and then go via the field edge to the restored house on a by-road. Take the path on the right of the house to join the Cleveland Way. To the right the path offers an unfolding panorama of cliffs ending on Cowbar Nab as it makes its way downhill past the hamlet of Boulby and on to the Cowbar road.

Follow this down to the little pier with its view across to

Staithes

Staithes. Retrace your steps to the footbridge over the little channel which provides extra shelter for fishing boats, and turn left along the narrow cobbled main street.

Opposite The Cod and Lobster turn up Church Street, even narrower. On the right is a plaque to Captain Cook and an alleyway just 18 inches wide. Church Street leads up to the cliff path which carries on first east and then south-east to Port Mulgrave where there is an attractive tea garden. Look down on the ruined quays of the port which was built in the middle of the nineteenth century to ship iron ore to the Tyne.

Note the cliff path by which the fishing boat owners have to carry their catch and all their needs. There is no road because the ore was brought by rail through a mile-long tunnel from Dalehouse at the foot of the valleys you have crossed.

Leave the cliff path to follow Rosedale Lane past the Ship

Inn to Hinderwell Church (with St Hilda's Well beside it), bear left to the village main street (A174) and cross it. Ahead of you a sign announces Porret Lane and on the left of the sign a narrow footpath takes you by gardens to a lane which, to the left, leads you to the crossing-keeper's house by the track of the old coast railway.

Just past this, the lane turns left, but take the field path straight ahead. Bear slightly right down the next field keeping the pleasant wooded stream on your left.

After crossing the metal bridge take the left hand path, climbing very steeply through woods. Cross the field, heading for the slight escarpment at the right-hand end of the ridge three-quarters of a mile distant.

Descend through beautiful woods down the sunken way (muddy) bearing to the left to reach a small masonry bridge with a pipe alongside. Bear left (still muddy) up the valley, gradually climbing to a stile leading into a field which may contain a bull with statutory cows.

In this case follow the edge of the wood to the left as far as the hedge then go up this to the end of the fence. The stile in the next hedge is just to the right of this line. One more narrow field and a stile leads you into the corner of the third and last field, very attractive with marsh marigolds, orchids and cowslips – but wet! Across the little marsh bear left, but keep right of the gorse, to reach a gate and stile on the Borrowby road at the top of the escarpment. Cross this and keep to the same contour for three-quarters of a mile to the Roxby road. Church and car are half a mile to the left.

Buses from Middlesbrough pass Ings Farm, the Staithes/Dalehouse crossroads and Hinderwell.

Walk 14
WASDALE HEAD CHURCH
CUMBRIA
9 miles

This superb circuit of Wastwater is intended to offer a greater challenge to those whose appetite for walking has been whetted by the shorter, less demanding excursions elsewhere in this book.

Although containing no climbing as such, the route along the screes which flank Wastwater's southern shore is most flatteringly described as 'difficult'. Do not assume that this three-mile section of the trip can simply be accomplished in the 'regulation hour': it involves a good deal of scrambling and negotiating boulders and will more likely take three times that time. Stout footwear is essential.

But for all these warnings, this is a superb excursion which takes the walker in the space of a few short miles all the way from the lush leafy greens of the Cumbrian coastal plain to the very foot of Scafell Pike, England's highest mountain.

Wasdale elicits other superlatives, too. In Wastwater it has the deepest lake in the country, and in our objective, in Wasdale Head, what is claimed to be the country's smallest church. Though other parishes might well challenge this latter claim, the seventeenth-century stone-built and wood-beamed church certainly is diminutive. Seating probably no more than two dozen people, it is little bigger than the average living room, but with all the trappings of its full-size brethren. The church is typical of many isolated places of worship in the Lakeland valleys.

Wasdale has also sired some famous sons, such as Jos

WASDALE HEAD CHURCH

1 mile

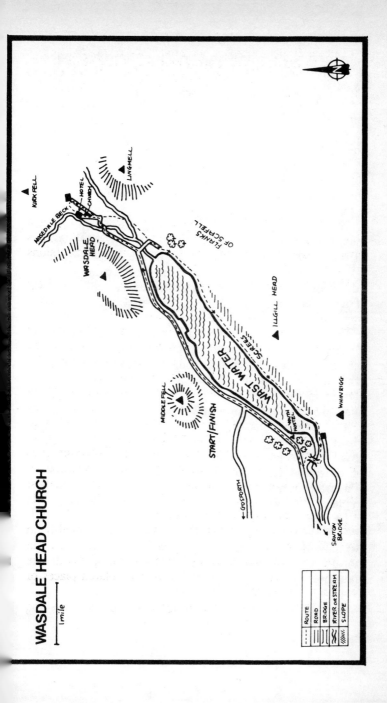

KIRK FELL

MOSEDALE BECK

HOTEL
CHURCH

LINGMELL

WASDALE HEAD

FLANKS OF SCAFELL

MIDDLE FELL

ILLGILL HEAD

SCREES

WAST WATER

WHIN RIGG

START / FINISH

GOSFORTH

NETHER WASDALE

SANTON BRIDGE

	ROUTE
	ROAD
	BRIDGE
	RIVER or STREAM
	SLOPE

Naylor, one of our greatest fell-runners. More subjective is the claim of the dale to have raised the world's biggest fibber. Will Ritson, once landlord of Wasdale Head Hotel, earned the accolade through the absolute whoppers he would tell visitors from the towns. One of his most famous tales concerned the dale's giant turnips which were so big that the locals, having quarried them for Sunday dinner, would use their remains for sheep and cattle sheds.

Although he died in the 1890s, the tradition of fibbing lives on in Wasdale and in 1974 Copeland Borough Council formalised it with an annual competition to find the world's biggest liar.

Wasdale can be approached by road only from the west, leaving the main A595 coast road at Gosforth, in the shadow of the great blot on the landscape of the Sellafield nuclear power complex, or leaving that same road further south and edging into Wasdale from Eskdale round the end of the fells. If dependent on public transport, consult the Mountain Goat bus company at Ambleside.

Park near the junction of roads from Gosforth and Santon Bridge, the last on the road up the dale. There is no defined parking area but choose your spot wisely and carefully somewhere along this stretch. It is suggested that the excursion be started in the morning to give you a refreshment stop at Wasdale Head and allow a full afternoon for the return trip.

The walk begins, following the road towards Wasdale Head. Look out for those making the trek along the far shore, small and insignificant against the enormity of the scree, a backdrop which contributes to the fantastic deep hue of Wastwater. The lake owes its physical depth – nearly 260 feet in places – to the power of a glacier scouring out a deep valley in its descent from the heart of the mountains.

The lakehead is reached after about two miles and the road is followed another mile to Wasdale Head. After a break at Wasdale Head, where there is a climbing shop and general store and where the hotel bar has photographs of the pioneers of British rock climbing on nearby Great Gable, the route is continued by passing to the rear of the hotel to the edge of

~ Wastwater ~
~ Yewbarrow ~ Great Gable ~ Lingmell ~ Scafell Pikes ~ 1/4.

Mosedale Beck. Appreciate, but do not cross, the typical Lakeland packhorse bridge and continue along the path (often wet) to the right of the stream.

After a short distance the path divides. Take the right fork which follows the edge of a tributary beck and becomes eventually a ramblers' 'motorway' to Sty Head pass and the climbs on Great Gable. After a quarter of a mile leave the path through a gate into the attractive yard of Burnthwaite farm, on your right. Return towards the little church about 500 yards distant along the farm road.

Note the huge piles of stones which can be seen at some field boundaries; when fields were cleared of glacial debris, there were more rocks than could usefully be incorporated into the walls. The church is simplicity itself, quite in keeping with its surroundings, and the churchyard has the obligatory yew trees.

75

Continue to where the farm road joins the 'main' road by the car parking area and follow the road a short distance to where the Eskdale bridleway leaves it through a gate on the left as the road bears right.

Follow the track which heads for the lakehead, about half a mile distant, keeping the campsite on your right. The route fords Lingmell Beck but this will not usually pose any problem. It joins the Wasdale Hall farm track at a wooden bridge over Lingmell Gill.

From here follow the signposted route to the shore through the copse, the Scafell path leaving to the left.

When you reach the lake, if you wish to bathe, here is the place to do so as this is the only part of the lake bottom which does not shelve steeply.

The shore path is easy going at first but gets steadily more difficult: the only advice is to keep on course, staying on the path at all times. When the bouldery section is reached, the more nimble can proceed relatively easily by leaping from boulder to boulder rather than clambering round each one.

Continue until the scree is left and the path leads to a footbridge over the River Irt. Cross the river and follow its bank the short distance to the road. Turn right, passing the Youth Hostel on the mile or so back to the starting point.

Walk 15
DOVE COTTAGE
CUMBRIA
5 miles

There are two poles to the magnetic attraction of the Lake District, which draws visitors in their thousands. One is the wild grandeur of its rugged fells; the other, the idyllic beauty of its sheltered wooded shorelines.

In capturing in verse the latter's serene qualities early in the eighteenth century, William Wordsworth and those he inspired brought to the public eye attractions which led to the foundation of a tourist industry which has its roots in Victorian times.

This walk is a pilgrimage to Grasmere, at the very heart of the Lakes, where Wordsworth lived in a succession of rented houses for 12 years before moving to nearby Rydal, where he died 37 years later.

Those early years at Grasmere saw the creation of most of his best-known work and, fittingly, the village became his final resting place. Today, his modest Dove Cottage home is a museum with many manuscripts and memorabilia of the poet, his wife Mary, sister Dorothy, and his friends, including the essayist Thomas De Quincey, a later occupant of the house. Dove Cottage is open daily, except Sundays, March to September, also on Sunday afternoons from April.

Also to be seen in the village are the church, with the Wordsworth family graves and that of Hartley Coleridge; Heaton Cooper's studio; and the perfumery. Above the village to the west is Wordworth's later home, Allan Bank.

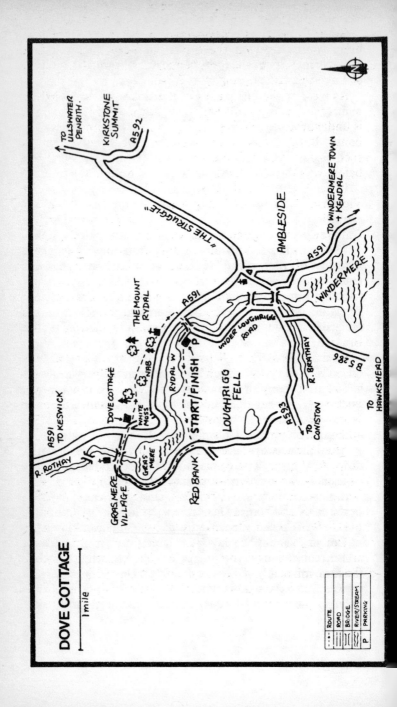

Grasmere remains a stronghold of the traditional Cumbrian sports, held on the third Thursday after the first Monday in August, and is the venue for the annual exhibition of Lakeland artists, usually in April.

As most of the low passes in the Lakes are occupied by main roads, it is often difficult to find a route for a walk which is undisturbed by traffic; one which provides fine views is a bonus. But our walk to Grasmere via Loughrigg Terrace is such a route, although it became popular many generations before cars drove walkers off the main routes.

It has been sneered at as 'an old ladies' walk', but the Victorian ladies showed judgement. Before that it was for centuries a Sunday walk to church at Grasmere, when Ambleside was without a church of its own.

The starting point for the walk is a new car park on a side road just off the main A591 Ambleside-Keswick road as it enters Rydal. Buses provide a service from Ambleside. Alternatively, non-drivers may walk the mile and a quarter from Ambleside by taking the footpath from Church Street, across the park to join the Under Loughrigg by-road at Miller Bridge.

From the car park, walk up the metalled track, past a series of cottages, the last of which boasts a superb show of gentians if you time it right. Provided conditions are not too wet underfoot, spring is ideal for the walk as there are fewer visitors and the gentians will be joined in bloom by bluebells, azaleas and Wordsworth's golden daffodils.

After the woods there is a choice of paths, one striking down to the shore of Rydalwater, the other following the edge of the wood on to Loughrigg Terrace. The latter is the better choice by virtue of the fine views over the lake, none better than that from an old slate quarry across the lake north to Nab Scar at the southern extremity of the Helvellyn range.

The path is easy to follow, keeping a near-level course around the 400 foot contour. As it bends leftwards, opposite the little hill of White Moss which separates Rydalwater and Grasmere, there is another fine view along Grasmere to the Lion and Lamb on Helm Crag, a mile to the north of the lake.

—Dove Cottage, Grasmere—

The path leads out on to a minor road at the steep Red Bank (those following the lower path round the shore of Rydalwater will miss most of this). Follow the walled road, with its pleasant gardens, all the way to Grasmere village, about a mile. It can get busy on holiday weekends.

As you enter the village, Allan Bank is on the left, the church on your right. Follow the road to the right, across the bridge and for a quarter of a mile or so until it reaches the main Keswick road almost opposite Dove Cottage.

After visiting the cottage, the return route begins via the narrow road which rejoins the main road the other side of White Moss. But after a bare quarter of a mile, turn left along a track (the second exit from the road on the left). Like Loughrigg Terrace, this track – and the bridleway it becomes after half a mile – runs level along the hillside, partly through woodland. Below the path, on the right, is Nab Cottage, where De Quincey lived and Hartley Coleridge died.

Don't be put off by the fact that this was to be Wordsworth's last walk, as he caught pleurisy and died. After all, he was 80, and it was quite early in the year!

The path emerges eventually at the head of Rydal hamlet, with its hall and The Mount, Wordsworth's home from 1813. By the time he moved there, he had become a national celebrity and was visited not only by writers, but also by Queen Adelaide, the widow of William IV, and many more humble sightseers who, it is recorded, by 1845 were queuing up in their carriages to meet the poet.

In 1970 a descendant of Wordsworth bought the house, refurbished it with family belongings and portraits and opened it to the public. The garden is very much as it was in the poet's time and has fine views over Rydalwater. Dora's Field, Wordsworth's only property, is magnificent in daffodil time and the house and garden are open in summer. The return walk is completed by continuing to the main road, turning left, and walking the few hundred yards to the Pelter Bridge car park.

Walk 16
RAVENGLASS & ESKDALE RAILWAY
CUMBRIA
2½ or 4½ miles

The attraction of the Ravenglass and Eskdale Railway for visitors is almost as old as Lake District tourism itself. Although it began life in 1876 as a 3 foot gauge railway to serve the iron mines which helped meet the demands of industrial boom days, when it was rescued from financial ruin and converted to 15 inch track in 1915, it was promoted as 'the world's smallest public railway'. Behind the idea was Wynne Bassett-Lowke, credited with the invention of the hobby of model railways.

Threatened with sale for scrap, it was again rescued by enthusiasts in 1960, since when it has gone from strength to strength and now carries around 250,000 passengers a year.

La'al Ratty as the line is affectionately known, is not only an attraction in itself, with its handsome little steam engines (one of which earned the line a £1,000 Steam Heritage award for technological innovation in 1986), it also gives access to one of the most attractive Lakeland valleys.

Although road access to upper Eskdale is dramatic – the view from the top of Hardknott Pass is stunning – many motorists will be disinclined to tackle the steady one-in-three gradient and tortuous hairpins, particularly in summer when there's a good chance of meeting oncoming traffic at the worst possible spot.

There are other road routes into Eskdale, but the recommended alternative is to travel by car or British Rail to Ravenglass and to take Ratty. The line runs all the year

RAVENGLASS & ESKDALE RAILWAY

N

1 mile

START/FINISH

IRTON RD
STATION

TO
RAVENGLASS

THE GREEN ST.

RIVER ESK

SIGNED BRIDLEWAY TO BOOT

RUIN

BECKFOOT STATION

DALEGARTH ST.

DALEGARTH HALL

STEPPING STONES

STANLEY GHYLL

	ROUTE
	ROAD
	BRIDGE
	RIVER/STREAM
	RAILWAY
	GATE or STILE

round, but there are considerable seasonal differences in frequency. For details telephone Ravenglass 226.

The Ravenglass and Eskdale Railway Co Ltd publishes a compilation by the renowned Alfred Wainwright of ten walks to be enjoyed in conjunction with a ride on the railway; a glance at the Ordnance Survey map will reveal many more possibilities. The one chosen for this book is a short but very attractive walk close to the banks of the Esk.

There is ample parking at the two termini, but motorists should use commonsense if you wish to start your trip from another station. The suggested starting point for our trip is The Green, roughly two-thirds of the way along the seven mile rail route. There is a public car park nearby at Eskdale Green. From Ravenglass, take the A595 north and turn right at the first available turning, after about two miles. The station is a little south of Eskdale Green on the road up the dale from Santon Bridge.

Leave the station, turn right and follow the road past the George IV, take the right fork (the Ulpha road) and continue to the bridge over the Esk. Pause to gaze into the beautiful clear waters of the Esk, so unlike the murky peat-laden rivers of many upland areas.

Take the bridle path on the left, signposted to Boot, Stanley Ghyll and Upper Eskdale. Follow the river bank for about half a mile until faced by two gates where the route leaves the water's edge briefly. Take the right-hand gate, marked with a small green bridleway notice, carefully negotiating the probably boggy area just beyond, and cross the field to the gate at the far side.

Here are the remains of an old farmhouse, and you can still see the neat cobbles of what was the farmyard. Beyond the farm, take the fork in the path leading to the river bank – an ideal spot for a picnic – and follow the new path along the bank until it veers inland into the wood. The track here is made of huge stone slabs – the hallmarks of an old pack horse route, although the author has not authenticated this deduction.

The wood is a magnificent mixture of mature native and

'Laal Ratty", Eskdale-

exotic species, including huge wellingtonia, the tall red-barked conifers so popular in country parks of this period. As the white house comes into view in a clearing ahead and to the left, take the right fork in the track, bringing you past Dalegarth Hall, behind the wall on the left. Note its splendid chimneys.

The track here passes a shallow little rocky escarpment on the left before reaching a 'crossroads'. Go straight on here through the gates, following the Upper Eskdale bridleway sign. Cross the clearing, go through the gate and into the wood, crossing the stream by a footbridge and emerging again into meadow.

At the far side of the meadow cross the stream and follow the path to the left, signposted to St Catherine's Church. The path takes you down through the trees to a gate which leads to stepping stones across the Esk. Cross the river and take a look at the plaque in the wall which reads: 'I will lift up mine eyes unto the hills.' This, unusually, is connected with a memorial on the other side of the wall, within the churchyard.

If the river is running too high for a safe crossing, return to the track and follow it a mile upstream to Doctor Bridge. Return via the footpath on the far bank, noting the site of the old branch railway crossing of the river, and St Catherine's holy well on a small plateau above the path. Both are about a quarter of a mile east of the church.

The church itself was rebuilt late last century on a site dating back to the Cistercians. Look inside for the tombstones of Tommy Dobson and Willy Porter. They were huntsmen of the Eskdale and Ennerdale pack and of greater renown than the legendary John Peel whose name lives on today further and wider thanks to the song which surely everyone must learn at school.

To return to the railway at Dalegarth station simply follow the walled track to the side of the church, keeping to the right fork to bring you through the farm. At the Boot crossroads take the main road left down the dale and the station is few hundred yards on the right.

Walk 17
CARTMEL PRIORY
CUMBRIA
4½ miles

The Cartmel Fells and the peninsula they occupy form a rather neglected appendage to the Lake District. Main roads avoid it because of the obstacles formed by the wide estuaries of the Kent and the Crake/Leven.

Only the Cumbrian Coast railway, which crosses these on long viaducts, carries through-traffic and offers fine sea views – but the attractive hinterland is hidden. This was not always the case: stage coaches made the direct journey from Lancaster to Ulverston across the sands, a precarious undertaking which several times ended in catastrophe because of the powerful tidal bore. In Cartmel, road signs still give misleadingly short distances to Lancaster and Ulverston via the sands.

The beautifully enclosed market place in Cartmel village, in which you can sit enjoying food and drink, is more continental than Cumbrian (its designation since local government reorganisation in 1974), and suggests a much bigger market town. Over a bridge is a 'mini' cathedral, part of the great Augustinian priory founded in 1188.

Thanks to repairs and restoration in the seventeenth century it has been saved for our enjoyment. In the soaring style of the twelfth and thirteenth centuries, it must be one of Britain's most impressive parish churches: the tower over the central crossing, with its belfry amazingly set at 45 degrees to its base, is an unmistakable landmark. The church, particularly its carved woodwork, is worth close study; look also for

CARTMEL PRIORY

1 mile

B5278
HAVERTHWAITE,
ULVERSTON

HILL MILL

HOSPICE TO GRANGE STATION

CARTMEL

PIT FARM

PRIORY

ALTERNATIVE ROUTE

HEAD-LESS CROSS

HOLKER HALL

CEMETERY

CARK HALL

B.R. TO BARROW

CAUSEWAY TO ULVERSTON

P

BOARBANK HALL

CARTMEL STATION (CARK)

CAUSEWAY TO LANCASTER

START/FINISH

HUMPHREY HEAD

- - - -	ROUTE
= = = =	ROAD
≡≡≡≡	BRIDGE
~~	RIVER/STREAM
▪▪▪▪	RAILWAY
P	PARKING

N

the loaf of bread set out daily in the north aisle for the poor.

The priory is more than a parish church; it is also the setting for a music festival and ambitious and unusual flower festivals.

After the priory itself, the most conspicuous architectural survivor is the gatehouse, a massive tower which separates the market place and Cavendish Street. In its time it has housed the court, prison, school and more recently a candle factory. It is now National Trust property but free entry is usually possible; art exhibitions are often held there.

Further exploration of the village is worthwhile as there are several interesting domestic buildings, and the little river is particularly attractive at the North Bridge, approached along Cavendish Street. The circuit can be completed through the priory grounds. Before entering the grounds, walk a few yards further towards the main road and see a small stream which flows northwards from a spring at Well House, in the opposite direction to that of the nearby Eea. This is the basis of the legend that the founding monks had to search for a site between rivers with contradictory flows.

Another attraction of this walk is Holker Hall, two miles further down the valley. Set in an extensive deer park, parts of the house date back to the sixteenth century. Once home of the Dukes of Devonshire, it is still occupied by other members of that family. As well as the park with its herds of deer, there are woodland walks and gardens with some immense tree heathers.

The parts of the house open to the public (from Easter to the last Sunday in October) are usually among the later additions. There is a motor museum, cafe and shops, but what brings most of the crowds are the special events, like the Lakeland rose show, hot-air balloon and light aircraft rallies.

Our walk to Cartmel starts at Cark and Cartmel station and motorists should park at Cark village on B5277/8 a short distance north of the station.

Follow the road into Cark and turn right, passing Cark Hall on your left and take the minor road to your right, climbing a mile to Boarbank Hall, now a nunnery. From this

- Cartmel -

road there are fine views south over Humphrey Head and the sands to Morecambe and north-west over Cartmel Sands to the hills behind Ulverston and beyond.

At the cross-roads beyond Boarbank turn left through Templand to drop into Cartmel by the Headless Cross.

To reach Holker, follow the metalled road across the race course and continue on the track with Seven Acres farm buildings slightly to your right; after passing through a wood take the right fork, keeping about 100 yards below High Bank Side Farm. Another half-mile will bring you onto the B5278 opposite the hall.

A possible extension is to begin from the station at Grange, from where the walk to Cartmel is about five miles return, and hilly, but in one direction you could cross Hampsfield Fell by way of the Hospice, a nineteenth-century shelter with a viewing platform on top – you *might* see Snowdonia, or Snaefell on the Isle of Man.

The access to the fell from Grange is by a narrow enclosed footpath leaving the road from the mini-roundabout opposite the railway station; the footpath is about a quarter of a mile on the left. The limestone fell is criss-crossed with rights of way. On a day of fine visibility there seems no good reason why the walker should not strike south from the Hospice, bearing right towards Cartmel to enter the village via Pit Farm, off the Grange road to the north.

Walk 18
DENT
CUMBRIA
4 miles

The 1974 reorganisation of local government in England, born of all the distant wisdom of the accountant and the statistician and with little regard for local allegiances and geographic commonsense, did have some benefits. A definite advantage as far as the author of this book is concerned is the annexation by the new county of Cumbria of parts of the old West Riding of Yorkshire lying west of the Pennine watershed. This gives our northern walkers the chance to sample the delights of some of the limestone country of what are still generally termed the Yorkshire Dales.

Dentdale – within the Yorkshire Dales National Park but for administrative purposes part of South Lakeland – is one of the most beautiful in the national park and, because it is relatively inaccessible, one of the quietest. The tumbling waters of a tributary of the River Dee in its tranquil upper stretches are said to have inspired a pensive and 'pre-industrialist' George Armstrong in his study of water referred to in the description of the Cragside walk in this book.

Further down Dent, as the dale is more locally known, is Dent Town (so called to distinguish it from the dale) which makes a worthy goal for our walk. Once a bustling community of close on 1,800 people it now has a permanent population of around a third of that figure. Its old houses and very unusual cobbled street – fashioned from unshaped stones which were extensively relaid in recent years – make the township well worthy of its status as a Conservation Area.

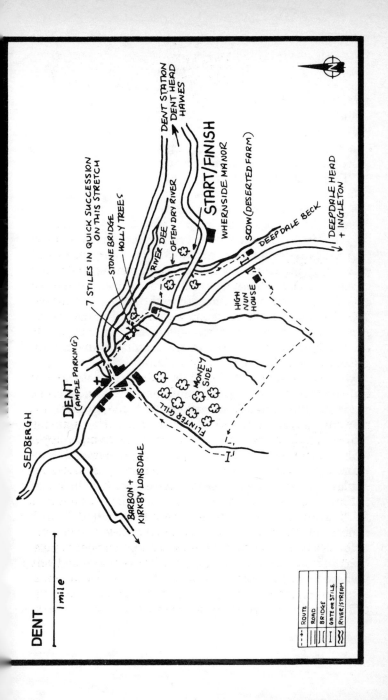

Its major claims to fame are its best-known son, Adam Sedgwick – the nineteenth-century father of modern geology in whose memory a great block of Shap granite is sited on the main street – and its terrible knitters. These were so called not because they were bad at their craft but because of an older meaning of the word which indicated the great speed with which they worked, at home or even while tending sheep or cattle, producing clothing for the army for use in the Continental wars in the eighteenth century.

Dent is difficult to reach by public tansport. Dent station – served twice daily at the time of publication – is four and a half miles from the township and some three miles from the starting point for our walk.

The start is at the abandoned corn mill at Millbridge which is on the road along the south, or so-called 'money side' of the dale. Driving from Dent, look for where the road crosses Deepdale Beck about 500 yards past the Ingleton fork.

There is limited parking space by the old mill. Alternatively, drive another 500 yards and park near Whernside Manor, run by the Yorkshire Dales National Park as a general outdoor activity centre. The house is reputedly not only home to three ghosts, but its eighteenth-century slave-owning occupants – the Sill family – are suggested by local historian Kim Lyon to have inspired Charlotte Bronte in creating the central characters in *Jane Eyre*, while Emily Bronte's Heathcliff in *Wuthering Heights* was based on a no-good orphan boy, Richard Sutton, adopted by the Sills, who later bought the manor. Mrs Lyon's findings are hotly contested, but those interested in the argument should be able to find a copy of her account at the Lyons' caving shop in Dent.

Starting the walk proper at Millbridge, take the stile on the south side of the road immediately to the west of Deepdale Beck. Walk through the wood along the sluice beds of the old mill and follow the track up the bank to the right to where it emerges into meadow land.

Bear left and pass the left-hand end of the wall ahead. Keep to the path as it follows the side of a sloping field, cross two

-Dent-

stiles and pass to the right of the abandoned farmhouse of Scow.

The route turns sharp right above the farm; negotiate four gates at the Ingleton road, then cross directly over the road and take the bridleway signposted to Barbondale. After a good steady three-quarters of a mile climb along this broad stony track, Nun House Outrake, a junction is reached with the old green track known as the Occupation Road. Bearing left, this heads for Deepdale Head, but our path follows the sign for Barbon, a level walk giving superb views over the dale.

After rather more than a mile the track kinks left over Flinter Gill and the hillside begins to bear left towards Barbon. Look here for the gate on the right which brings you onto a steep lane leading directly to Dent village.

To return, leave the village by the main road up the dale,

signposted to Hawes at the George and Dragon opposite the Sedgwick stone. Take the stile on the right just before the bridge and follow the footpath across the meadow, keeping to the right of the stream. Cross a succession of stiles, after the seventh of which the footpath crosses the stream by a stone bridge before picking its way through mature holly trees and crossing a small tributary.

Keep on the right of the wall as you approach the farmhouse, follow the detour to the right and cross straight over the lane to where the footpath follows the right-hand side of the meadow.

The path joins and keeps to the bank of Deepdale Beck and you may notice how the river bed can be quite dry – a classic feature of limestone country where the water has found a different route underground.

Discarded millstones in the wood indicate your imminent arrival back at the starting point. Corn was last ground here at the Over Mill (which most likely replaced the original Nether Mill as the population grew) in the first half of the last century, giving reason to reflect that Dent was presumably by then well past its heyday and its populace long since departed for the industrial towns of the West Riding.